DATE DUE

NO 9 '95			
MR 11 '03			
OC 13 08			

DEMCO 38-296

*Culture-Centered Counseling
and Interviewing Skills*

Culture-Centered Counseling and Interviewing Skills

Culture-Centered Counseling and Interviewing Skills

A Practical Guide

PAUL B. PEDERSEN
AND ALLEN IVEY

PRAEGER

Westport, Connecticut
London

Library of Congress Cataloging-in-Publication Data

Pedersen, Paul.
  Culture-centered counseling and interviewing skills : a practical
guide / Paul B. Pedersen and Allen Ivey.
    p. cm.
  Includes bibliographical references and index.
  ISBN 0-275-94668-1 (alk. paper). — ISBN 0-275-94669-X (pbk. :
alk. paper)
  1. Counseling. 2. Interviewing. 3. Cross-cultural counseling.
4. Culture—Psychological aspects. I. Ivey, Allen E. II. Title.
BF637.C6P335 1994
158'.3—dc20   93-15372

British Library Cataloguing in Publication Data is available.

Library of Congress Catalog Card Number: 93-15372
ISBN: 0-275-94668-1
    0-275-94669-X (pbk.)

First published in 1993

Praeger Publishers, 88 Post Road West, Westport, Connecticut 06881
An imprint of Greenwood Publishing Group, Inc.

Printed in the United States of America

The paper used in this book complies with the
Permanent Paper Standard issued by the National
Information Standards Organization (Z39.48-1984).

10 9 8 7 6 5 4 3 2 1

Contents

Preface

This book is directed toward students and professionals who are studying about counseling, teaching counselors, doing research on counseling topics, administering programs with a counseling function, or delivering a direct service as counselors. The skill-based focus of this book is guided by a three-stage developmental sequence, including multicultural awareness, knowledge, and skills.

The first chapter emphasizes the importance of culturally learned assumptions in counseling. The focus is on developing and becoming more aware of how cultural similarities and differences shape the counseling interview.

The second chapter develops a cognitive framework in the Cultural Grid to organize knowledge about culture in a counseling relationship. The focus is on understanding and working with cultural systems in a meaningful way.

The third chapter introduces four culturally different dimensions based on a fifty-five-country database that demonstrates patterns of similarities and differences across cultures. Four synthetic cultures are constructed from the four research dimensions to provide a databased framework of cultural differences.

The fourth through the tenth chapters emphasize specific micro-skills as those skills are modified to fit each of the four synthetic cultures. By learning to reframe each micro-skill to each of these four synthetic cultures, the counselor's repertoire for each micro-skill is expanded to fit the complex and dynamic needs of culturally different client populations: Alpha (high power distance), Beta (strong uncertainty avoidance), Gamma (high individualism), and Delta (strong masculine).

By understanding differences among clients from a culture-centered framework, it becomes possible for persons to disagree without one being right and the other wrong. The culture-centered framework allows persons with culturally different behaviors to maintain their cultural differences while focusing on the common ground of culturally similar expectations for fairness, trust, or success for the counseling relationship. The culture-centered framework acknowledges the importance of both cultural differences and cultural similarities by defining culture inclusively to include all potential roles or identities a person may have based on ethnographic, demographic, status, or affiliations. The counselor is trained to identify the complex and dynamic salience of the client's culture as it changes.

By the time the reader successfully completes this book, he or she will be able to:

1. Identify culturally learned assumptions that shape a counseling interview;
2. Interpret a client's behavior in the client's cultural context;
3. Adapt counseling techniques to four culturally contrasting synthetic cultures;
4. Develop a repertoire of at least four culturally different adaptations for the basic micro-skills of counseling.

The culture-centered approach to counseling presumes that all counseling, to some extent, is multicultural. It also presumes that the client and counselor's behaviors are determined by culturally learned assumptions and understanding those assumptions accurately is essential for effective counseling. Culture is not treated as an exotic or specialized aspect of counseling, but rather as the heart and soul of any and all counseling relationships.

Each chapter will be introduced by identifying primary and secondary objectives for the chapter. Practical examples and exercises will be provided within each chapter to demonstrate and rehearse the skill being described. The end of each chapter provides an outline of the key ideas explained within the chapter. A summary exercise for demonstrating competence with the skill is provided at the conclusion of each chapter.

The micro-skills described in chapters 4 through 10 are an abbreviated version of Ivey's micro-skills, combining some of the skill areas which are dealt with separately and in more detail elsewhere. By identifying four alternative applications of each micro-skill, the reader will be guided toward matching additional skills and counseling strategies as well to the specific needs of culturally different people. The synthetic cultures provide a framework for each counselor to construct an approach to counseling that fits the client's cultural identity.

ACKNOWLEDGEMENTS

Studying culture teaches us that we are never alone. We are always surrounded by thousands of persons, living and dead, who have had significant influence on our lives. The difficulty in listing some of those individuals is the danger of inadvertently leaving others out. Persons from counseling as well as many other professional disciplines have helped us focus on multicultural aspects across disciplines and fields. Many of the significant leaders and advocates of multiculturalism were not counselors, but developed ideas about culture that are essential to a culture-centered approach to counseling.

Frequently those progenitors were ethnic minority authors whose works have still not received the recognition they deserve.

The target population we hope to reach with this book are not just the readers who buy and use it. We would like to dedicate this book to the clients of counseling who benefit directly from trained counselors and who are the clear ultimate focus of our training. May your clients be empowered by what you read and find common ground more easily through your efforts in a multicultural future.

We would like to acknowledge the hard work of Mildred Vasan at Greenwood Press who encouraged us and made the job easier. We would also like to thank Sue Kelly for helping us transfer our ideas and rhetoric into a printed manuscript. Finally, we would like to thank our family, colleagues, students, and many friends who provided suggestions, encouragement, and support when we needed it.

Paul Pedersen
Allen Ivey

Culture-Centered Counseling and Interviewing Skills

Part One

Culture Centeredness

Culture controls our lives. We may attend to our culturally learned assumptions or we may ignore them, but in either case, these assumptions will continue to shape our decisions. Culture is not something outside ourselves, but, rather, an internalized perspective that combines the teachings of every significant person or group we have experienced, read about, or heard about and from whom we have learned something. When individuals try to understand their own or someone else's culture, it is understandable that they are frequently overwhelmed by the complexity of the task. Each of us then "belongs to" a thousand or more cultures, any one of which might become salient or most relevant depending on the time, the place, and the situation.

Many researchers, teachers, trainers, and service providers are so overwhelmed by the complexity of culture that they choose not to include it in their analyses of research data, educational activities, or other psychological services (Pedersen et al., 1989). Unfortunately, ignoring the influence of culturally learned assumptions means giving up freedom, power, and intentionality in our personal and professional lives. It is a little like speeding in a car down a busy street without having your hands on the steering wheel. Attending to culturally learned assumptions, on the other hand, provides a basis for more accurate analyses, more complete comprehension, and a more appropriate matching of our own and others' behaviors with the culturally learned expectations behind those behaviors.

The culture-centered approach to counseling is not new. The idea of making culture a central concern to counseling grows out of G. Kelly's personal construct theory (1955). Kelly said we are motivated by everything that has happened to us and that teaches us what to do or what not to do. Through these collective experiences we develop personal constructs, and differences in personal perspective are explained by the individual experiences people have. Our past has helped us develop constructs that we use to predict the future.

Consequently, people with similar constructs get along better than people with dissimilar constructs. In many ways Kelly's notion of personal constructs resembles the broad definition of culture used in this book. Like personal constructs, culture is within the person, develops as a result of accumulated learning from a complexity of sources, depends on interaction with others to define itself, changes to accommodate the experiences in a changing world, provides a basis for predicting future behavior of self and others, and becomes the central control point for any and all decisions.

Many of the approaches to skill training have emphasized changing behaviors. Culture-centered counseling skills focus on the culturally defined assumptions that shape and direct behaviors.

Person-centered approaches presume that individuals decide and function independently from their culturally defined context and therefore tend to neglect the cultural forces that define the person.

Problem-centered approaches presume that if externalized problems can be solved, the counseling is successful, without recognizing the sometimes necessary function that "apparent problems" fulfill in a culturally defined context.

Behavior-centered approaches presume that a person's behaviors constitute data without reference to the cognitive framework used to interpret and direct those behaviors.

Situation-centered approaches explain the world through transactions and interactions of collectivities without regard to the individual's cultural identity aside from any "particular" culture system or group.

Each of these approaches shares an area of overlapping concern, and that is the concept of "meaning."

Each system explains the world in such a way that people's behavior has meaning. The culture-centered approach to counseling focuses on cultures as the teachers of meaning. Culture-centered counseling skills focus on the culturally learned expectations and values that control behavior and have been learned through ethnographic, demographic, status, and formal and informal affiliations accumulated from a lifetime of experiences. Each individual's unique combination of shared behaviors, situations, problems, and systems is a product of the cultures on which this approach is centered.

Skills-based approaches to counseling have been proven to train counselors perhaps more effectively than any of the alternatives (Pedersen, 1986). The culture-centered approach suggests that skill training is focused on the culturally defined context in which skills must be learned and eventually applied. This book on culture-centered counseling skills attempts to identify patterns of interpretation, explanation, and meaning that have explicitly or implicitly grounded the alternative approaches to understanding human behavior. If the book is successful, the reader will recognize and label culturally learned assumptions in which the person already believed but never articulated. If this book works, readers will find practical insights to understand their own and others' behavior better. If this book is useful, it will help identify the construct "culture" as a valuable and underutilized resource to define the similarities and differences that unite and divide us not as exotic curiosities but as core values.

The focus of this book is on the complex and dynamic cultures we carry inside us which teach us the assumptions that shape our expectations and control our behavior. This approach separates cultural from personal facets of individuals. Each of us was born with a particular skin color at birth, but skin color itself is not cultural. The internalized meaning that our skin color has taken on for us and for others is cultural.

By focusing on the cultures within the person, appropriate skills can be adapted to that person's changing needs and identity at different times and places. A person's behavior, for example, only becomes meaningful data when it is connected to the culturally learned expectations that led to that behavior. A culture-centered approach seeks to interpret behavior by interpreting it within the context of culturally learned expectations, values, and the sources of that learning.

Synthetic cultures introduce a safe approach to examining cultural differences. Synthetic cultures provide examples of cultural values derived from real cultures but without their overwhelming complexity. Learning to deal with the limited complexity of synthetic cultures and their relationship to an individual's actual culture provides the basis for learning about the much more complicated cultures of the real world. Synthetic cultures provide a temporary laboratory in which culture-centered counseling skills can be safely nurtured and developed for transplantation later to real-world cultures.

The synthetic-culture approach presented in this book introduces four separate cultures: Alpha, Beta, Gamma, and Delta. These four extremes provide a framework to organize, classify, and analyze the range of similarities and differences in real-world cultures. The framework of synthetic cultures in the laboratory facilitates our understanding of real-world cultural complexity.

Individual ——————— Synthetic Culture ——————— Real World

The first step in developing culture-centered skills is to identify culturally learned assumptions in ourselves and others. Frequently these assumptions are so taken for granted that they are overlooked by the people making those assumptions. Our comprehension of reality is filtered through these culturally learned assumptions. Learning to recognize culturally learned assumptions is the first step in being able to manage them effectively. The first part of this book focuses on this.

The second step in developing culture-centered skills is to increase knowledge about particular cultures. The need for and uses of cultural knowledge and information become obvious if there is an adequate awareness of culturally learned assumptions.

The third step in developing culture-centered skills is to increase one's facility in managing or interacting with different cultures. Skills that are grounded in an appropriate awareness and accurate knowledge are most likely to be effective in multicultural situations.

In summary, this book provides a model based on awareness, knowledge, and skill for use in courses and training programs about multicultural issues. The synthetic cultures provide a mechanism for developing and rehearsing culture-centered skills safely. The synthetic cultures also incorporate the full range of verbal and nonverbal responses based on data from fifty-five countries.

The following chapters proceed from identifying culturally learned assumptions to knowledge about culture and finally to skills in managing multicultural tasks.

Chapter One

The Multicultural Three-Step

Major Objective:
To define a culture-centered approach to counseling and suggest ways to develop it.

Secondary Objectives:
1. To define culture as complex and dynamic.
2. To describe the developmental sequence from awareness to knowledge to skill in developing a multicultural awareness.
3. To identify problems and barriers to culture-centered counseling.

By the time you have completed this chapter you may be aware that multicultural communication is complicated but not chaotic. You will also have knowledge of the variety of multicultural training approaches now being used. Finally, you will have the skill to state your own assumptions about culture.

To help you achieve these, Chapter 1 begins with an exercise to help raise your awareness of specific cultural differences in the assumptions of people with different experiences. It continues with an overview of culture as defined in this book. A perspective on contemporary practices in multicultural training follows this discussion. The chapter concludes with an introduction to a particular training sequence for developing culture-centered skills.

EXERCISE 1.1

We live in a multicultural world of legitimate contrasts in values. This can be illustrated by contrasting two different but widely believed perspectives of educational objectives based on work by H. A. Thelen (1956).
Perspective A: "I want my child to be treated as an individual by teachers

who center their attention on the children and see themselves essentially as guides. Children are capable of planning and discussing their experiences, of being guided from within. The important thing is understanding and insight that leads to growth. I want them, through firsthand experience, to learn the meaning of freedom, to understand and be committed to a democratic way of life. But, above all, I want them to be adequate people, with a rich and ennobling subjective inner life; only thus can they achieve the creative spontaneity that is a person's most precious attribute."

Perspective B: "The teachers are instruments of society and are hired primarily because of their mastery in the sciences and the arts as arranged in school subjects. Their job is to give instruction and to communicate not single interesting facts but rather ideas organized in meaningful relationship to each other, as in a lecture. Teachers know the material to be covered, and it is their responsibility to plan in such a way that it will be covered. Teachers know that getting ahead in this world requires the ability to meet the demands of the community, and only through drill and practice can school achievement become part of one's habit pattern. Many of the important things in life were discovered by others and are learned through vicarious experiences dominated by these great authorities. Children are free to think as they wish, but in the objective world of action they must conform to the standards of the community."

Examine your perspective on education. Circle the number in the following semantic differential that best describes your own commitment to education.

individual	1 2 3 4 5 6 7 8 9 10	society
child-centered	1 2 3 4 5 6 7 8 9 10	subject-centered
guidance	1 2 3 4 5 6 7 8 9 10	instruction
discussion	1 2 3 4 5 6 7 8 9 10	lecture
pupil planning	1 2 3 4 5 6 7 8 9 10	teacher planning
intrinsic motivation	1 2 3 4 5 6 7 8 9 10	extrinsic motivation
insight learning	1 2 3 4 5 6 7 8 9 10	drill and practice
growth	1 2 3 4 5 6 7 8 9 10	achievement
firsthand experience	1 2 3 4 5 6 7 8 9 10	vicarious experience
freedom	1 2 3 4 5 6 7 8 9 10	dominance
democratic	1 2 3 4 5 6 7 8 9 10	authoritarian
subjective	1 2 3 4 5 6 7 8 9 10	objective
spontaneity	1 2 3 4 5 6 7 8 9 10	conformity

You have just increased your awareness regarding contrasting perspectives of education from two frames of reference. Perhaps you have also become more knowledgeable about your own perspective based on examining these two frames and more skillful in articulating your thinking about education. Where did your perspective come from? Who taught you the underlying assumptions on which that perspective is based? You may now want to ask a friend or two with whom you think you agree or disagree about what they believe are the aims of education. Usually we discuss topics like education without looking at the culturally learned assumptions that shape each person's perspective on that subject. The culture-centered approach begins with an awareness of culturally learned assumptions on which our beliefs are based.

OVERVIEW OF CULTURE

Broadly defined, the concept of culture includes the ethnography, demographics, status, and affiliations that have taught each person a framework of underlying assumptions. If, for example, someone were to ask you to define your culture, how would you answer? To begin with, your parents or ancestors may have come from a foreign country. In the census, you are listed as belonging to a particular ethnic group. You may add to the list of possible census answers your religion, your language, or some other demographic influence. Perhaps your social status, your level of education, or your economic level has also shaped your identity. On the other hand, perhaps your gender, age, or place of residence has made a difference. Finally, you might consider any one of the thousand different groups to which you are formally or informally affiliated, such as your family, organizations, or ideas in which you along with others like you believe.

Your culture includes all these elements, any one of which might become salient according to time, place, and/or situation. You are an individual, but you are not isolated from the many overlapping cultural circles of other individuals to which you belong. Your cultural priorities are complex and dynamic as the salient culture changes in each situation. Your culture is defined both by the ways you are similar to another person or group of persons and by the ways you are different and unique from every other person or group. By attending to both the areas of cultural similarity and those of cultural difference, you achieve a sense of your cultural identity in the social context of other persons and groups of persons.

Our culture teaches us everything we know about ourselves and the world around us. Our language, behaviors, rules, and ways of understanding others are all learned in a cultural context from those among whom we live. Culture provides a framework of assumptions for understanding and relaying that understanding to others. We do not always recognize the assumptions behind our behavior, but they are always there and always important.

Any attempt to reduce culture to esoteric categories of faraway people ignores the fact that, from their perspective, we are also faraway and somewhat exotic. We do not usually think of our own rules and behaviors as cultural, but rather describe them as normal. There is often an implicit assumption that there is a single standard for normal behavior without realizing how the criteria for normal behavior changes from time to time, place to place, and person to person. As you saw in the example showing different perspectives of education, societies differ in their emphases on the value of individualism or collectivism, dependency or independency, family-centered or social-centered environment.

By recognizing that our behavior is culture-centered, we can better understand both the similarities and differences among ourselves and others. Rather than emphasizing the process of communication, the culture-centered approach emphasizes the basic underlying cultural assumptions that determine our behavior, expectations, and values. If we overemphasize cultural similarities and presume that cultural differences are unimportant, we end up imposing a more powerful majority perspective on a relatively less powerful minority in the illusion of a melting pot. If we overemphasize cultural differences and presume that cultural similarities are unimportant, we end up stereotyping ourselves and others in an exclusionary polarization that is likely to result in a hostile militancy.

The term "culture-centered" encompasses both the range of similarities and differences among priorities and identities in a pluralistic society. There is a balance of similarity and differences in the culture-centered perspective. The concepts of cross-cultural, trans-cultural, and intercultural often imply a comparison of different cultures in which one is often implicitly judged superior and another inferior. All communication is to some extent culture-centered. For this reason, culture-centered counseling skills are not specialized approaches for dealing with exotic populations but generic skills for matching the variety of behaviors, expectations, and values that separate any one person from another but also unite them.

THE COMPLEXITY OF CULTURE

The most important characteristic of culture is its complexity. If you are asked to describe your culture, you might well find the question ambiguous and difficult to answer completely. If, on the other hand, you are asked to give the reasons your culture has led you to make a particular decision (e.g., to marry a certain person or remain single), the task would still be complicated but much less ambiguous. You might then consider demographic factors such as age and place of residence; status factors such as social, economic, or educational level; affiliations including both formal and informal memberships, beliefs, and life-style; as well as ethnographic variables such as nationality, ethnicity, language, and religion. In any case, you would have a very long list describing your personal cultural orientation to the decision you made. To get a clear idea of how culturally complex you are, match the adjectives that describe your behavior with the group that taught or encouraged you to do it in the following exercise.

To complete this exercise, follow these steps:

1. Go through the following list of adjectives and make a check in the "Me as I see myself" column by those that you feel describe you.

2. Go back through the list and think about the teacher or group(s) that either taught you or encouraged you to be that way. Write in the appropriate label for the ethnographic, demographic, status, and affiliation teacher or group(s) by the adjectives that you feel best describe their expectation of you. Not all adjectives will be applicable; not all will be positive.

3. Cultural teachers or culture reference groups might include ethnographic (nationality, ethnicity, religion, language), demographic (gender, age, place of residence), status (social, economic, educational), or affiliation (formal like a family group or informal like a shared idea/belief).

Adjective	Me As I See Myself	Cultural Teacher or Culture Reference Group
1. Adventurous		
2. Affectionate		
3. Ambitious		
4. Anxious for approval		
5. Appreciative		
6. Argumentative		
7. Big-hearted		
8. Competitive		
9. Complaining		
10. Critical of others		
11. Demanding		
12. Discourteous		
13. Distant		
14. Dogmatic		
15. Dominating		
16. Easily angered		
17. Easily discouraged		
18. Easily influenced		
19. Efficient		
20. Encouraging		
21. Enthusiastic		
22. False		
23. Forgiving		
24. Forthright, frank		
25. Fun-loving		

Adjective	Me As I See Myself	Cultural Teacher or Culture Reference Group
26. Give praise readily		
27. Good listener		
28. Helpful		
29. Independent		
30. Impulsive		
31. Indifferent to others		
32. Intolerant		
33. Jealous		
34. Kind		
35. Loud		
36. Neat		
37. Need much praise		
38. Obedient		
39. Optimistic		
40. Orderly		
41. Rebellious		
42. Resentful		
43. Responsible		
44. Sarcastic		
45. Self-centered		
46. Self-representing		
47. Self-satisfied		
48. Sentimental		
49. Show love		
50. Shrewd, devious		
51. Shy		
52. Sociable		
53. Stern		
54. Submissive		
55. Successful		
56. Sympathetic		
57. Tactful		
58. Teasing		
59. Thorough		
60. Thoughtful		
61. Touchy, can't be kidded		
62. Trusting		
63. Uncommunicative		
64. Understanding		

Adjective	Me As I See Myself	Cultural Teacher or Culture Reference Group
65. Varied interests		
66. Very dependent		
67. Well mannered		
68. Willing worker		

You can see how your own personal cultural orientation is complex but not chaotic. The adjectives that have contributed to your identity came from the cultural teachers or culture reference groups to which you belong. No single cultural category gives a complete description of you.

In the psychology literature, Bieri (1955), building on Kelly's personal construct theory, was the first to introduce the concept of cognitive complexity, referring to the elaborateness or simplicity of a person's personal constructs. Complexity was measured by distinguishing between persons who used many constructs and people who used few to interpret the world around them (Burger, 1990).

People with less ability to use complex constructs will depend on fewer interrelated categories to help them understand each different situation. This insight applies particularly to cultural differences. P. E. Tetlock (1985) demonstrated that the less complexity American and Soviet political leaders incorporated into their public statements, the less harmony in their relationships toward one another. He suggests that more cognitively complex leaders will be better able to see disputes from the other country's point of view. Other research (Burger, 1990) also suggests that more cognitively complex people are more sensitive to other people's perspective.

W. H. Crockett (1965) introduced a method for you to measure your own level of cognitive complexity.

EXERCISE 1.3: CROCKETT'S COGNITIVE COMPLEXITY TEST

1. Think of a person you like and a person you dislike. Take five minutes each to write a description of these two people, paying particular attention to habits, beliefs, ways of treating others, mannerisms, and attributes.

2. When you have finished both descriptions, count the number of different constructs you have used to describe each person. Any aspect of the person's personality or behavior counts (introverted, talks too much) but not physical characteristics.

3. Add the number of constructs together for your score. While the number of constructs is only a partial measure of cognitive complexity, this measure is widely used (Burger, 1990).

Cognitively complex persons are more persuasive and more likely to change their arguments depending on whom they are talking with, making it easier to match their arguments to different audiences. People with more complexity can better deal with ambiguity and are less likely to be anxious in unexpected or unstructured situations. Students with a low degree of complexity in their self-descriptions become depressed more easily (Burger, 1990).

THE DYNAMIC NATURE OF CULTURE

Not all of the memberships and affiliations comprising a person's culture are equally important at any one time or place. Each of the many groups to which we belong becomes more or less important for us depending on a given situation. Recognizing that we have a variety of different cultural identities or memberships available to us, we choose the combination most appropriate for each time and place. As we move from one setting to another, we adapt to the changing requirements in a dynamic, rather than static, definition of our identity.

H.J.M. Hermans, H.J.G. Kempen, and R.J.P. Van Loon (1992) present a theory in a "constructionist" perspective where the self goes beyond both individualism and rationalism and is focused on its contextual nature. Psychological processes are shaped by culture and history. Rather than describe the self in static and isolated terms, they describe the self as "dialogical," emphasizing cultural relationships. The self is a product of countless stories, experiences, and dialogically interacting selves. We construct our notion of reality just as we construct our notions of self out of our multicultural experiences. The self is our dialogical narrator, taking on a multiplicity of positions. The dialogical self contends that the same person may take on many different identities which may agree, disagree, misunderstand, understand, oppose, contradict, question, and even ridicule one another.

Other people occupy positions in this multi-self, which is both here and there at the same time. Every significant person you have met, read about, heard about, or thought about remains with you accumulatively to construct you as you now are. In counseling, clients will frequently report hearing what their parents or other significant people in their lives said to them at a significant point in time, and the client may even participate in imaginary discussions with those previous acquaintances.

We may think of self in the singular, but J. S. Brunner (1990) describes the self as "interpersonal," where different internal roles interact with a situation according to their own agenda and best interests almost as though there were many persons inside the individual. The description of self as singular has been a typically Westernized approach in contrast to a more pluralistic description in Asian literature (Sampson, 1989). Hermans, Kempen, and Van Loon (1992) synthesize the singular and plural definitions of self in a "dialogical" description of self-identity.

In order to understand culture, it is important to be aware of the constantly changing patterns of our own culture in relation to others. Different aspects become more salient at different times, and the effective communicator needs to match or even anticipate changes in cultural salience. Culture-centered training is an attempt to develop the capability to manage cultural complexity and respond appropriately to dynamic changes in cultural salience.

EXERCISE 1.4

Consider this: Jones is African-American and Smith is European-American. Can you describe an instance in which their less obvious cultural differences, like social position, education, or age, might be the most important variable in their relationship? Think back to Exercise 1.2.

Increased interest in culturally complex and dynamic approaches to training has resulted from changes in the political, social, and economic power balance of the world community. There is a need for culture-centered guidelines to manage the increasing contact between countries and cultures. The definitions of counseling and communication must accommodate a wide range of differences across cultures. This book is an attempt to meet those needs based on four general assumptions:

1. Counseling is strongly influenced by cultural biases favoring an individualistic perspective.

2. All relationships are multicultural to the degree that our identity is complicated by differences in socio-economic status, age, gender, lifestyle, and other significant affiliations of either the counselor and/or the client.

3. The culture-centered counselor will be able to mediate effectively between different cultural perspectives and communicate meaning accurately.

4. Culture-centered communication techniques are of value only to the extent that they contribute to a stronger rapport among people.

COMMUNICATION BARRIERS

A frequently made assumption is that reasonable, well-meaning people can communicate accurately with each other. Data and experience, however, suggest that this is not always accurate. There are barriers to communication that are rooted in culture, and these barriers may keep rational, well-intentioned people from communicating accurately with one another.

Each of us defines normal behavior according to our own culturally learned criteria, and to a greater or lesser extent, each of us defines normal behavior differently. To be a competent counselor in a multicultural setting, you need to be aware of your own cultural biases. In other words, you must be aware of your own cultural encapsulation (Wrenn, 1962, 1985).

Wrenn describes the culturally encapsulated person as someone who substitutes stereotypes for the real world, disregards cultural variations among other people, and dogmatizes technique-oriented definitions. Many counselors believe their job is to make people happier, experiencing more pleasure and avoiding more pain, rather than to help the client find a meaningful balance between the inevitability of pain and pleasure in their lives. Many counselors believe the techniques of genuineness, warmth, and empathy work in the same way across all cultures, making the technique more important than the culturally different persons to whom that technique is applied.

Encapsulation is the result of overdependence on a single cultural variable to the exclusion of any others. First of all, consider the variety of social system variables that teach perspectives of reality and identity. The most obvious cultural variables, such as nationality and ethnicity, may not be the most important. Gender, socio-economic status, life-style, job or professional role, and other functional roles or affiliations not only complicate one's cultural identity but construct separate identities as well, competing with one another in the internal dialogue of the person.

As noted earlier, we function both as individuals and as members of culturally defined groups in any given situation. This culturally constructed identity changes with the setting and topic under discussion over time. It is possible to work with a client from another culture on a problem that introduces additional sources of cultural influence, and in an environmental context that imposes its own unique cultural values. Therefore, you must begin by developing two very basic capabilities: (1) to identify greater numbers of relevant cultural variables at any given moment; and (2) to keep track of the constantly changing salience of cultural variables as the situation changes from moment to moment.

Commonly identified communication barriers include verbal and nonverbal language problems, interference from preconceptions and stereotyping, erroneous evaluation, and stress (Barna, 1982). Sometimes the organization itself acts as a barrier, preventing people from communicating accurately.

1. Assuming similarities instead of differences.
2. Verbal language problems occur when another person uses words you do not understand.

3. Nonverbal language problems occur through intentional or unintentional behavior, which is accurately or inaccurately interpreted by others.

4. Preconceptions and stereotypes can become so influential that you see and hear only what you expect, ignoring the real person in front of you.

5. Evaluation biases result from drawing premature conclusions of value judgments about other persons and/or situations before you have all the facts.

6. Stress barriers arise when you feel danger and try to protect yourself against a real or imagined enemy. Multicultural situations are often ambiguous and result in stress because you are not sure what others expect of you or what you can expect of them.

7. A. Pedersen (personal communication, 1985) identified another barrier of organizational constraints that arise when culturally different persons or groups want to communicate but the rules of the organization prevent accurate communication either intentionally, as in institutional racism, or unintentionally.

Later we will discuss the specific techniques to use when you encounter these barriers.

EXERCISE 1.5: THE IMPORTANCE OF SPEAKING OUT AGAINST RACISM

1. Identify a racist act that has occurred recently in your community (school, town, region, nation) and is widely known among the group.

2. Divide into two-person teams.

3. In each team one member will conduct an "opinion poll" of people passing by about the incident.

4. The confederate will approach the pollster at about the same time as another student who is responding to the survey.

5. Both students will be asked how they think the college/university should respond to the incident.

6. The confederate will answer first, giving a strong response against the instigators of the incident in half the cases or a strong response in their defense in the other half.

7. Hearing someone else express strong opinions either for or against racism will likely shape the bystander's opinion toward the strong views of the confederate (Blanchard, 1991).

8. Debrief the student, explaining the nature of your experiment. We do not want to encourage racism.

EXAMPLES OF CULTURE-CENTERED TRAINING:
AWARENESS

Training is an attempt to increase a person's options for being accurately understood in a wide variety of cultures. Culture-centered training must be responsive to the variety of cultures among those being trained. The benefits of training are measured by their relevance to real-life situations. The more alternatives or strategies an individual possesses, the more likely that right choices will be made in each different cultural setting.

A variety of multicultural training approaches have been used to prepare counselors and interviewers to work in other cultures (Brislin, Landis, and Brandt, 1983). These various approaches can be classified according to their emphasis on awareness, knowledge, or skill as the primary focus. Awareness requires the ability to see a situation from both your own and the other's viewpoint with accuracy. Several of the classic multicultural training approaches emphasizing awareness include experiential learning, cultural awareness, and specific cultural values clarification.

In experiential learning, participants "experience" the effect of similarities and differences by their own involvement in the training process. The assumption is that increased involvement in the life of another culture by experiencing it through direct or simulated contact will increase the accuracy of opinions, attitudes, and assumptions about the other culture. A trainer helps facilitate this involvement safely by helping the participants analyze the effect of their experiences. A trainer might use cultural immersion, field trips, or role-playing as examples of experiential training.

Cultural immersion requires an individual to live and work in another culture and learn by experience. The Peace Corps has frequently relied on immersion in real or simulated cultures as a training method. Early German missionaries in Sumatra, Indonesia, would frequently be separated from their families and sent to a remote village for the first year of their term to learn the language and local ways of doing things. When they became fluent in the language and familiar with the culture, they were reunited with their families.

Field trips provide less traumatic experiential training. Many aspects of a host culture can be learned but not "taught." The field trip places participants in situations where they are able to observe a culture in its own context. It is often easier for a host culture resource person to demonstrate a skill or activity than it is to describe it in a classroom. A trainer provides structure to the field trip so the participant/observer can learn from the experience. The field trip can have a specific focus to illustrate or challenge attitudes, opinions, and assumptions from one or both cultures.

In role-playing, an individual learns about another culture by assuming the role of a person from it. The experience of becoming someone else often changes a participant's level of awareness. The trainer must provide careful structures to guide learning through role-play, both to provide a safe context in which a role-player might take risks and to generate insights about the other culture.

Experiential approaches to training are often expensive and require highly skilled trainers as well as cooperative host culture resource persons. The value of experiential approaches depends on creating a safe context for participants, who may otherwise experience a great deal of stress which could be counterproductive to training and at times even dangerous to the participant.

Culture-general approaches are primarily useful in helping people articulate their own implicit cultural attitudes, opinions, and assumptions. In a culture-general self-awareness approach, the values of a people's home culture are contrasted with those of many other cultures. The emphasis is usually on areas of general similarity and difference. Our own cultural values are frequently so familiar that we are not explicitly aware of them. In some cultures, for instance, the importance of individualism would be an example of an implicit value that is different from the implicit value of collectivism in many other cultures. R. S. Brislin et al. (1986) provides a cultural-general framework through critical incidents.

The "contrast American" training design (Stewart, 1971) emphasizes generalized cultural awareness. A resource person is coached to behave in ways typically in contrast to those of the American trainee in a role-played interaction. The general patterns of contrasting attitudes, opinions, and assumptions are then evident in the role-play and can be studied in detail.

Cultural-specific approaches—being trained in the specific values of a particular other culture—is another example of culture-centered training. Culture-specific training is usually limited in focus to the particular group with which the trainee will have most contact. Learning the language of a host culture, for example, is an important culture-specific way of learning about its attitudes, opinions, and assumptions.

A variety of other awareness training approaches focusing on the individual trainee (self-awareness) and the home culture (culture awareness) emphasize similarities and differences by contrasting cultural systems with one another. The emphasis is always on reevaluating the trainees' attitudes, opinions, and assumptions about their own and other cultures.

EXAMPLES OF CULTURE-CENTERED TRAINING: KNOWLEDGE

Knowledge training is another popular focus for culture-centered training. It means having correct and sufficient information about one's own as well as the target cultures. The most frequently used ways of increasing a person's knowledge and comprehension of another culture are books and audio/visual media.

Classroom training emphasizes lectures, group discussions, written materials, and media presentations to help trainees increase their information.

Trainees need to have factual information about the host culture to understand their own role as outsiders. These facts might relate to the socioeconomic and political structures of a country or culture, the climate and physical setting, decision-making styles and habits, and the values underlying daily behavior.

The facts themselves will be most useful if trainees are highly motivated to learn the new information and see an immediate relevancy for increasing their knowledge. For that reason it is important that these factual data be based on an awareness of why they are important. Without sufficient awareness, trainees are not likely to be motivated toward gathering increased information. Well-informed trainees will also be best prepared to document their awareness of cultural similarities and differences. With the appropriate preparation, trainees can become highly motivated to increase their information through fact-oriented training.

In attribution training, a participant learns to explain behavior from the host culture's viewpoint. Given a critical incident or paragraph-length description of an event, the participant is asked to choose between several alternative explanations attributed to the incident. One of these is more right than the others for specific reasons. Participants are coached to select the accurate and appropriate attribution through practice, analyzing a series of critical incidents. There is an assumption that the trainee will learn implicit patterns of decision making through attribution training which will generalize to unfamiliar situations and incidents encountered in the host culture. Brislin et al. (1986) have developed a book of critical incidents using attribution training methods.

The most well-known practical application of attribution theory is the "culture assimilator" developed by H. C. Triandis. Much research has been done on the culture assimilator in a wide variety of culturally different settings. There is probably more data on this than on any other single culture-centered training approach (Triandis, 1983). Culture assimilators provide a structured series of incidents and alternative responses, where, in each set, one response is more accurate and appropriate than the others. Explanations are provided for the rightness or wrongness of each choice. To the extent that culturally accurate and appropriate attributions can be determined for each situation, the culture assimilator has been extremely successful.

EXAMPLES OF CULTURE-CENTERED TRAINING: SKILL

Skill is being able to do the right thing. Adequately trained people will have the skills to match the right method to the right situation in the right way. Skill approaches most frequently associated with culture-centered training relate to cognitive behavioral modification and a variety of interactions more affectively oriented.

Cognitive behavioral modification training is based on identifying rewards or reinforcers in the cultural context. In this way, trainees can adapt their more culturally familiar habits to the unfamiliar culture. If a new set of rewarding or reinforcing consequences can be matched with the required behaviors in an unfamiliar culture, trainees are more likely to make a satisfactory adjustment. This approach depends on knowing the principles of learning theory well enough to teach participants about their use.

Affective-oriented training usually depends on structured interaction between participants and host culture resource people in an actual or simulated setting. In the process of rehearsing the skill being learned in a safe context with feedback from an already skilled facilitator, the participant is actually able to display skilled behavior with increased sophistication. The key element to interaction training is the feedback on participants' success or failure as they attempt to use new skills.

Microskill training, or the idea of dividing more general skill areas into smaller units, is perhaps best represented by A. E. Ivey (1988), who divides counseling into specific attending behaviors, influencing skills, and integrative skills. By being taught a progressively more difficult series of microskills, the trainee builds on foundation skills toward more advanced and complicated skills. There is more empirical research data supporting the effectiveness of microtraining than on any other skill-building method.

Structured learning is another social behavioral method widely used in skill building (Goldstein, 1981). It identifies practical skills and competencies needed to perform a necessary function for a particular cultural group in a specific setting. The skill is presented and discussed before it is demonstrated to trainees with the opportunity to clarify any confusion. The skill is then rehearsed by the trainees in role-played situations with feedback from a supervisor or trainee, and finally it is transferred to the real world outside the training setting through implementation in actual practice.

Skill training leads us to assume a foundation of international or multicultural attitudes, opinions, and assumptions that have been reevaluated from several cultural perspectives. Skill training also assumes a large amount of factual knowledge and information to document the similarities and differences across cultures.

The identification of culture-centered counseling skills is the focus of this book. An activity will be presented later on skill building from four different cultural perspectives using a combination of the methods described in this chapter.

EXERCISE 1.6: STRENGTHS AND WEAKNESSES

Can you list some weaknesses or problems you might anticipate if your culture-centered training program objectives were based exclusively on:

1. awareness development?
2. knowledge accumulation?
3. skill building?

What would be the consequences of culture-centered training programs that:

1. began with knowledge accumulation as the first step?
2. began with skill building as the first step?
3. left out awareness development?

In evaluating your own or some other culture-centered training program, how would you know that the basic problem is a lack of:

1. awareness, or wrong assumptions?
2. knowledge, or wrong facts and information?
3. skill, or the inability to use awareness and knowledge appropriately?

FROM AWARENESS TO KNOWLEDGE TO SKILL

Awareness, knowledge, and skill are all necessary elements of culture-centered training. This three-stage sequence, or developmental model, was designed by the staff of a National Institute of Mental Health training project at the University of Hawaii from 1978 to 1981 titled "Developing Inter-culturally Skilled Counselors" (DISC) (Pedersen, 1981).

Awareness provides the basis for accurate opinions, attitudes, and assumptions. People become aware of the intentional priority they give to selected attitudes, opinions, and values. They are able to compare and contrast their own viewpoint with alternative points of view accurately. They are able to relate and translate their own professional role to a variety of cultural settings. They are aware of culturally defined constraints and opportunities in each culturally different setting. They are aware of their own resources, skills, and limitations for working in other cultures.

In the same way, knowledge provides the documentation and factual information necessary to understand another culture. People have the knowledge to describe the complete system of another culture at the local, national, and regional levels accurately. They have knowledge of the literature regarding the other culture. They know the research about relations between their own and the other culture. They know where to go to get more information about the other culture. They also know key resource people from the other culture who can help them understand it.

Finally, skill provides the ability to do something with the awareness and knowledge people have accumulated. Trained people become skilled in planning, conducting, and evaluating the culture-centered training of others. They are able to assess the needs of the other culture accurately. They are able to work with interpreters and cultural informants from the other culture. They can observe and understand behaviors from the other culture. They are also able to interact, counsel, interview, advise, and manage a task or responsibility in it.

A report by the Education and Training Committee of Division 17 (Counseling) of the American Psychological Association has become a model for culture-centered training of counselors. This report identifies minimal multicultural competencies for training them in their beliefs/attitudes (awareness), knowledge, and skills (Sue et al., 1982).

The basic three-stage developmental framework of competencies first published in the Sue, et al., (1982) article were elaborated in the American Counseling Association Professional Standards. The notion of these professional competencies was to match each counselor goal with culturally appropriate attitudes and beliefs, knowledge, and intervention strategies.

This framework has proven to be a useful framework to evaluate and measure competencies of individual counselors, to identify problems in agencies or organizations, organizing training workshops, developing course material on multiculturalism, and even preparing to work with a culturally different client in direct service. When the assumptions are clear and appropriate in one's cultural awareness, then the need for specific and accurate knowledge is apparent. When you are sure that your assumptions are appropriate and you have all the information available, you can easily identify the research or information gaps where skills are needed. The three stages flow from one to another in a smooth developmental sequence.

Culturally aware counselors are:

1. aware of their own cultural backgrounds,
2. aware of those assumptions and value biases socialized by that cultural background,
3. comfortable with cultural differences between counselors and clients, and
4. sensitive to circumstances that might require referral of a client to a culturally similar counselor.

Culturally knowledgeable counselors have:

1. an understanding of the sociological role of minorities in the United States,
2. specific knowledge about the culture of their clients,
3. a clear and explicit knowledge of the generic counseling literature, and

4. knowledge of institutional barriers that prevent minorities from using mental health services appropriately.

Culturally skilled counselors can:

1. generate a wide variety of verbal and nonverbal responses appropriate to a wide range of cultures,
2. both send and receive verbal and nonverbal messages accurately and appropriately to or from culturally different people, and
3. change the system or institution on behalf of a client when the individual is right and the system is wrong.

A DEVELOPMENTAL CULTURE-CENTERED TRAINING MODEL

Each of the training models discussed previously is uniquely appropriate for specific multicultural training objectives. It is important for the trainer to select the appropriate method for each situation. By dividing these more popular methods according to their primary emphasis on awareness, knowledge, or skill, we have attempted to identify their primary function. We can now examine a developmental framework for culture-centered training that combines other valuable training modules.

The following approach to culture-centered training differs from the previously described approaches in that the three components are emphasized in a developmental sequence. This sequence will need to:

1. establish clear awareness, accurate and appropriate attitudes, opinions, and assumptions about the target culture,
2. acquire knowledge or comprehension based on accurate and sufficient information about the target culture, and
3. develop skill to apply appropriate awareness and accurate knowledge for taking effective action in the target culture.

By maintaining a balance of awareness, knowledge, and skill in culture-centered training, the trainer should be better able to match the right method with each situation. The importance of building on the sequence of stages toward informed and intentional multicultural skill is the focus of this three-stage developmental model.

The skill-building plan for the rest of the book will follow a sequence of stages. The first emphasizes awareness of culturally learned assumptions. It focuses on the assumptions that counselors might make about an issue and helps them verify their appropriateness in the form of right questions. Through increased awareness, they are better able to evaluate and, if needed, change an attitude or opinion toward others. An example of awareness would be the judgment about the goodness or badness of a person, place, or thing. They might believe, for example, that teenagers are self-centered and thoughtless. The attitudes, opinions, and assumptions they make tend to predispose them toward a positive or a negative conclusion regarding that other person, place, or thing with or without their conscious awareness.

The second stage in this sequence emphasizes knowledge, or comprehension, and provides an individual tool kit to build accurate and appropriate assumptions for identifying right answers to the right questions with information resources. An example of knowledge would be seeking answers to the basic questions: who? what? when? where? why? Once they have made their evaluation, the increased information or knowledge they gather will help them confirm or disconfirm it. By increasing their knowledge or amount of information, they are better able to comprehend meaningful relationships, circumstances, and implications about others.

The third stage in this sequence emphasizes skills or the ability to take action, using both awareness and knowledge in the synthesis. Awareness and knowledge become the resources upon which skill draws. The skills stage builds on both an intentional awareness of assumptions and on accurate information needed for taking appropriate action. By increasing their skill based on right knowledge and right awareness, they are more likely to act appropriately toward others. Skill is defined by their competency, capacity, capability, efficiency, or talent to achieve the level of effectiveness they intend. Once they have established and documented their assessment of a situation through accurate information, skill permits the appropriate management of the resources at their disposal.

Counselors need to develop specific counseling and interviewing skills based on appropriate awareness and accurate knowledge to address such areas of multicultural concern as verbal and nonverbal language, preconception and stereotyping, evaluation biases, and the stress barriers mentioned earlier.

If any of the three stages of awareness, knowledge, or skill is missing from their training, difficulties are likely to arise. If they neglect awareness, they are more likely to build on wrong or inappropriate assumptions. If they neglect knowledge, they may be inaccurate in their description of a situation. If they neglect skill, they may well be changing the situation in counterproductive directions.

EXERCISE 1.7: SUCCESS AND FAILURE

Identify an example where you were successful in a multicultural setting directing a project, developing a relationship, making a decision, or making a difference in some other way.

1. What were the underlying assumptions you made, and how did they contribute to your success?
2. What knowledge or information did you have, and how did it contribute to your success?
3. What action did you take, or what did you do that contributed to your success?

Identify an example where you were unsuccessful in a multicultural setting directing a project, developing a relationship, making a decision, or making a difference in some other way.

1. Were your assumptions about that situation appropriate?
2. Did you have accurate knowledge and information?
3. Did your skills build on appropriate awareness and accurate knowledge?

LIMITATIONS OF CULTURE-CENTERED TRAINING

In attempting to understand complexity, we develop simplified models that can be explained and understood but that reflect only selected aspects of our reality. Our commonsense rationality requires that we construct simplified models of complex reality in order not to be overwhelmed. If we behave rationally with regard to the model, then we assume the behavior is appropriately generalized to the real world. The danger is that we confuse the labels with reality. We have little tolerance for ambiguity. We move quickly to sort, order, and predict emerging patterns from the confusion. This acknowledgment of human weakness must always be kept in mind while doing culture-centered training. It is important to recognize the consequences of effective training both for the participant and the host culture.

Training will have an impact on the trainee's family and community. These consequences may be either positive, enhancing adjustment to a host culture, or negative, weakening the trainee's traditional cultural values.

The trainers need to anticipate any problems that might arise from changing the consumer's home, work, and/or community setting. In many cases, a successful training program may set off an unanticipated chain reaction or events that might be potentially harmful to the participant.

The trainer needs to anticipate any potential effects of implementing changes to bridge the gap between the training situation and real life. The successful generalization of training requires thinking through its application. Potential changes in personnel policies, supervisory roles, and approved ways of conferring status will need special attention.

Training needs to incorporate examples of good and bad ways of integrating awareness, knowledge, and skill. Respect for traditional culture is essential in the broader application of training with sensitivity to organizational constraints.

Training that includes local people from both the host and home cultures through informal and formal contact is most likely to succeed. Unintended learning through casual contact provides a network for maintaining the benefits of training for both cultures.

CONCLUSION

Much of culture-centered training is intended to increase a person's ability to manage complex information. By perceiving the world from a narrow frame of reference, we ignore the complex reality around us in the illusion of simplicity. Many phenomena can best be understood from a variety of different perspectives. Theories of cognitive complexity suggest that people who are more cognitively complex are more capable than others of seeing these multiple perspectives. Research in adult development likewise suggests that cognitive complexity is related to broader and more advanced levels of development. Cultural complexity also suggests that we can best be understood from a variety of different coexisting cultural perspectives.

By now it should be apparent that culture, as we broadly define it, includes the full range of ethnography, demographics, status, and affiliations in a complicated but not chaotic pattern unique to each person for each decision and situation. We share the same patterned response with others just as we share the same identity according to our role at the time. For that reason, it is possible to train people for work in multicultural settings by helping them recognize the patterns and increasing their repertoire of appropriate responses. The separation of awareness, knowledge, and skill is an attempt to provide a systematic framework in which to teach and understand the meaning of culture in our normal multicultural situations.

You have now had the opportunity to examine your own assumptions about culture and compare them to others'. In addition, you should be able to explain the most popular culture-centered training approaches in terms of their emphasis on awareness, knowledge, or skill. Finally, you should be able to articulate your own assumptions about culture and culture-centered training.

KEY IDEAS

1. Culture is complex.
   Culturally learned patterns control our lives.
   Culture is defined by our assumptions.
   Behaviors must be interpreted in a cultural context.
2. A culture-centered approach to counseling is necessary.
   Individual differences are birth characteristics.
   Cultural differences are learned from birth.
   Synthetic cultures provide a contrasting framework.

3. The multicultural three-step developmental sequence.
   Awareness requires recognizing culturally learned assumptions.
   Knowledge requires facts and comprehension.
   Skills require the ability to do the right thing.
4. An overview of culture.
   A broad definition goes beyond ethnographic boundaries.
   Culture salience changes according to time and place.
   All learning is culturally defined and comprehended.
   Culture includes both similarities and differences.
5. The complexity of culture.
   Culture includes a broad spectrum of identities.
   Culture-centered approaches are based on personal constructs.
   Complexity is your friend, not your enemy.
   Cognitive complexity is a positive characteristic.
6. The dynamic nature of culture.
   The constructionist perspective of dialogical selves.
   Cultural salience is constantly changing.
   All counseling is to some extent multicultural.
7. Communication barriers.
   The dangers of cultural encapsulation.
   Identity is culturally defined.
   Barriers can presume similarity, whether verbal or nonverbal.
   Stereotypes, evaluation, stress, and organizational constraint.
8. Examples of culture-centered training.
   Training increases accuracy in selecting alternatives.
   Awareness training includes experiential, immersion, field trips, role-
   playing, and laboratory exercises.
   Knowledge training includes classrooms, attribution training, and
   analyzing information.
   Skill training includes cognitive or behavioral modification, affective
   orientation, microskills, and structured learning.
9. From awareness to knowledge to skill.
   A three-stage developmental sequence.
   Awareness provides accurate opinions and attitudes.
   Knowledge provides documentation and facts.
   Skill is the ability to use awareness and knowledge.
10. A developmental culture-centered training model.
    First, establish an accurate and appropriate awareness.
    Second, acquire accurate and sufficient knowledge.
    Third, develop accurate and appropriate skills.
    The three stages provide a meaningful sequence.

11. Limitations of culture-centered training.
     There is a danger in all simplified models.
     Training may have negative consequences.

12. Conclusion.
     Managing complex information is the goal of training.
     Culture should be defined broadly, not narrowly.
     Counselors need to know their assumptions.

EXERCISE 1.8: TESTING YOUR AWARENESS, KNOWLEDGE, AND SKILL

Check your ability to identify the use of awareness, knowledge, and skill in the following critical incidents:

1. Circle the words that indicate attitudes, opinions, or assumptions of goodness or badness in this situation: The person with whom you are traveling, a friend from back home, seems to be turning into an "ugly American," being condescending in the treatment of others, suspicious of being cheated, concerned that nothing is "clean" enough, and generally obnoxious toward non-Americans. You want to help the person make a better adjustment both to be helpful and to avoid embarrassment. You take the person aside for a little talk.

2. Circle the words that indicate the presence or absence of knowledge or factual information that documents accuracy or inaccuracy in this situation: You are in a mixed group of new acquaintances from different countries. Elections have just been held with political parties divided along Protestant and Roman Catholic lines. Discussion is extremely intense and likely to erupt into violence. You are not well enough acquainted with the issues to recognize which of the people in your group belong to which political party and/or which religious group. One of the leaders in the group asks you for your opinion.

3. Circle the words that indicate an ability or skill being applied in this situation, and judge for yourself whether the skill is being applied in the right way: In spite of your best efforts to learn the foreign language of a country you are visiting, you find yourself very inadequate in your ability to express yourself. The people with whom you talk on the street seem very impatient and somewhat irritated by the way you do violence to their language. You refuse to use English, even though their English is very adequate, and you are beginning to resent their lack of sympathy with your attempts to speak their language. You catch yourself becoming unreasonably angry with a complete stranger who doesn't understand you when you ask him a simple question.

Chapter Two

The Cultural Grid and Culture Systems

Major Objective:
To describe a conceptual framework called the "Cultural Grid" for distinguishing between personal and cultural aspects of intrapersonal and interpersonal relationships.

Secondary Objectives:
1. To present the broad range of social system variables which shape values, expectations and behaviors of individuals intrapersonally.
2. To describe the importance of shared expectations for interpreting different behaviors in interpersonal relationships.
3. To suggest practical applications of the Cultural Grid in culture-centered counseling.

Culture includes both similarities and differences. The most obvious function of multicultural awareness, knowledge, and skill is to prevent overemphasizing or underemphasizing any single cultural aspect, which would result in stereotyped and inaccurate perspectives. By understanding both within-group and between-group differences, it is possible to discover and assess the importance of any cultural aspect for a more reliable and valid perspective. The purpose of this chapter is to introduce a Cultural Grid for increasing a counselor's awareness and knowledge of cultural systems. This will provide an important foundation for the culture-centered skills that follow.

CULTURAL SYSTEMS

Cultural systems provide an important means for increasing a person's awareness and knowledge about how culture works. A cultural system is an interacting combination of influences that defines a personalized network of people who share the same assumptions, attitudes, and opinions. Culture is an internalized pattern more or less shared by people within a particular group at a particular time and place. Cultural systems describe the network of relationships among individuals and the groups of people with whom they share a particular perspective.

Understanding cultural systems and their underlying assumptions helps explain how two people—beginning with different culturally learned assumptions—can disagree without one necessarily being right and the other necessarily being wrong. To the extent that two people share the same cultural background, their assumptions are likely to be similar, and to the extent that they represent different cultural backgrounds, their assumptions will possibly be different. These assumptions and attitudes find their expression in the contrast between fact and inference.

For an accurate assessment of a multicultural situation, it is important to separate fact from inference. A statement of fact concerns something that actually exists, occurs, or otherwise has an objective reality that can be proven by the testimony of a neutral witness. A statement of inference is a conclusion that goes beyond the fact or event observed. We frequently assign expectations, attitudes, motives, or values to someone else which could probably not be verified by an objective witness. Although inferences are a normal and necessary part of reasoning, we can get into trouble by confusing them with facts.

Statements of fact are (1) made after observation or experience; (2) confined to what we observe; (3) limited in any situation; (4) after observation, the closest to certainty we will ever get; and (5) important in attaining agreement. Statements of inference (1) are made any time—before, during, or after observation; (2) go beyond what we observe; (3) are unlimited in any situation; (4) represent only some degree of probability; and (5) can easily result in honest disagreement.

In order to clarify the difference between fact and inference with regard to cultural systems, it is useful to analyze a critical incident case study involving multicultural elements, such as this:

You are a participant in an international group with an African-American male leader. Some in your group see the leader as very authoritarian, succeeding in dominating, planning, and controlling the activities of the group. He is seen as very jealous of any threat to his control. Some other members of the group are able to tolerate his domination, but you personally find it increasingly impossible and tend to agree that this leader has problems. The other group members have begun looking toward a Caucasian female member of the group with considerable international experience for advice and guidance about what to do. She believes that the leader is doing a bad job, and she represents a threat to his authority. You encourage her to sit down and have it out with the leader for the sake of the group as well as yourself. The preceding critical incident can be analyzed by answering the following questions regarding relevant facts and inferences.

1. Which cultural variables are mentioned explicitly and factually in the preceding critical incident? Ethnographic (African-American, Caucasian), demographic (male, female), status (leader, participant), affiliation (group member).

2. Which cultural variables are implied or inferred in the preceding incident? We might infer that the Caucasian woman with international experience is educated, older, or perhaps wealthy. We might also infer that the African-American leader is educated and has affiliations that led him to be assigned leader. As we picture both persons in our mind's eye, we no doubt will be making other inferences about their cultural background.

3. What facts do we know about the participants' behavior? Some members of the group approached the female Caucasian member for help. You encouraged her to talk to the African-American leader.

4. What inferences are we likely to make about the participants' behavior? We are likely to infer that the African-American leader is domineering and that the group is turning to a Caucasian female for advice, even though all the evidence for those conclusions is hearsay.

5. Can you describe the situation from the viewpoint of both the African-American male and the Caucasian female? The leader might infer that he was under attack by certain group members, including yourself, who refused to recognize his rightful authority and expertise and who are probably prejudiced against him for being African-American. He might perceive the Caucasian female as an ambitious person who is herself seeking power. The Caucasian female might infer that she needs to rescue the group from the leader's domination, especially if she is being encouraged to take over control by other group members like yourself. She might believe that she has as good or better credentials and, therefore, a right to take power.

You will notice how much these different viewpoints are based on inferences and how much they contrast with one another. The inferences drawn from this situation are more likely than the facts to shape each person's perception and guide decisions about what to do next. Remember, to the extent that two people share the same cultural background or systems, their inferences and assumptions are more likely to be similar, and to the extent that they represent different cultural backgrounds or systems, they are less likely to be similar (LeVine and Campbell, 1972).

EXERCISE 2.1: CASE EXAMPLES FOR ANALYSIS

Using the above example as a model, try analyzing this multicultural critical incident:

Your new Pacific Islander friends insist on borrowing things from you as a wealthy American student and neglect to return them unless you ask for them back. They appear much more casual about ownership of personal belongings than you would like and assume that they have a right to your things as your friends. You try to set an example by not borrowing anything from them, but they continue to borrow from you and do not acknowledge the subtle hints you make. They seem to be using you to their own advantage, although among themselves they seem to have developed a satisfactory arrangement.

1. Which cultural variables are mentioned specifically in the incident?
2. Which cultural variables are implied or inferred?
3. What facts do you know about the participants' behavior?
4. What inferences are you likely to make from each participant's behavior?
5. Can you describe the incident from the viewpoint of each participant?

Compare your responses to the above five questions with the responses of another person, and explain the similarities and/or differences.

CULTURAL VALUES

Personal value systems are related to how people distinguish fact from inference. It is important to distinguish between the objective and subjective in the study of cultural similarities and differences (Triandis, 1972). Objective culture refers to social indicators such as name, ethnicity, gender, age, education, kinship relations, economic background, and occupation. These indicators of culture can be observed directly in a society.

Subjective culture includes social indicators such as feeling, believing, conceiving, judging, hoping, intending, expecting, valuing, and other ways of giving meaning. These mental states are more difficult to observe directly. We may frequently overemphasize the objective, visible indicators of cultural difference and thus fail to attend sufficiently to the more subjective, less visible indicators. Cultural values are examples of subjective culture.

Values define the boundaries of cultural systems and are therefore very important in training people to communicate across cultural boundaries. A cultural value is an idea that does not require external or outside evidence to be accepted as true. Groups of individuals share more or less similar values or beliefs that help them communicate with one another and explain their similarities and differences. These values become a yardstick for groups to measure an individual's degree of belonging to it. Groups with different value systems are likely to experience conflict or disagreement because they will experience the same event from the viewpoint of contrasting assumptions. For children and adults, for instance, homework can be a source of conflict. Children may view homework from a narrow short-term perspective: drudgery that takes away from their free time. Parents, on the other hand, may take a broader, long-term perspective, seeing homework as necessary for their children's success and as a reflection of their ability to enforce self-discipline in their children.

Contrasting cultural dimensions separate groups of individuals from one another. We can look at these differences at three levels of interpretation: international, ethnic, and social role. At the international level, cultural differences separate people according to their country's role in world affairs, language, upbringing, and national allegiance. At the ethnic level, cultural differences separate groups labeled as African-Americans, Chicanos, Native Americans, Asian-Americans, and European-American ethnics from one another as well as from a loosely defined "American" dominant culture. At the third level of social role, groups or individuals may define themselves as sharing the same culturally subjective viewpoint as administrators, housewives, hardhats, or club members.

The difficulty with the traditional perspective of values is that cultures are often more complicated than it seems to imply. Cultural variables are like traits or dispositions that are characterized by constancy, even though they may appear to vary from time to time, place to place, and person to person. For example, an individual with a generally kind disposition may act un-The same variability holds true for people who share the same cultural values and priorities. Rather than mirroring one another, they may behave differently while maintaining the same general cultural disposition. Clearly defined, absolute cultural categories tend to bend the data to fit a more or less rigid framework of standard typologies for convenient but simplistic definition.

THE INTRAPERSONAL CULTURAL GRID

The Cultural Grid defines culture as comparatively more complicated and dynamic. Culture is broadly defined by boundaries that include the social system variables introduced in Chapter 1: demographic (age, gender, place of residence), status (social, educational, economic), and affiliations (formal and informal) to different groups in addition to ethnographic categories (nationality, ethnicity, language, religion). In the Cultural Grid approach, culture is also dynamic in that the emphasis or salience of a cultural variable will continuously shift from one situation to another, becoming more or less important in terms of the person's cultural identity. In the framework of the

Cultural Grid, culture is described more as an interaction of constantly changing personal and cultural variables.

The cultural grid combines personal features of individual cognition with social system group variables in describing a personal-cultural orientation. A. Pedersen and P. Pedersen (1985) and A. Hines and P. Pedersen (1982) developed the Cultural Grid to identify and describe the cultural aspects of a situation, to form hypotheses about cultural differences, and to explain the outcomes of multicultural interaction. The Cultural Grid is an open-ended model that matches social system variables with patterns of behavior, expectation, and value in an orientation to each event that is both personal and cultural. In this way the Cultural Grid provides a means of understanding and predicting a person's behavior, given knowledge of culturally salient expectations and values in a situation.

In the counseling literature, there has been a marked tendency to presume that complex factors must be simplified to obtain concise criteria for prediction and decision making. For that reason, the entire constellation of potentially salient social system variables shaping our behavior is condensed to a few, obvious categories such as nationality and ethnicity. Our natural tendency is to construct simplified labels of complex reality in order to manage that reality more conveniently without necessarily considering the complexity. When we behave rationally with regard to the labels we have just created, we assume that behavior may be appropriately generalized to the real, outside world. It is dangerous to confuse labels with reality, especially when considering culture.

We know that appearances count in first impressions. When you think of a person of a certain age, job, income level, gender, or life-style, you see a picture in your mind's eye of what you expect that person to look like. You are likely to judge those you meet in that actual role if they do not fit your expectations. These stereotypes oversimplify our thinking by limiting to a few rigidly defined characteristics our criteria for making judgments.

Sometimes the expectations of the counselor and the client are quite different. This preference for simplicity, then, often masks both the degree of similarity and of difference between them. Without understanding culturally learned expectations, it is impossible to interpret behavior by either accurately. Culture has made a profound contribution to our understanding of human behavior by complicating explanations of personal development and interpersonal contact according to different times, places, and people.

Imagine yourself walking up to a stranger to introduce yourself. What are your expectations of how that person will react? What are that person's expectations of how you will act? It is difficult to know what to expect. Now imagine a situation where you are in conflict with another person whom you know slightly but not well. Each of you will respond according to your expectations. Expectations are very important in a relationship, but they are also very difficult to identify accurately. There are several problems in accurately identifying expectations (Rubin, Kim, and Peretz, 1990):

1. People react according to how they perceive a situation and not according to how it is, and false perceptions will lead to false expectations.
2. There is never enough information to make a completely informed judgment, so expectations are usually based on too little.
3. If people do not know one another, their expectations are likely to depend on stereotypes, rather than facts.
4. As people interact, their expectations will change according to how accurate and appropriate others are acting.
5. We tend to perceive selectively, favoring evidence that supports our established expectations, which leads to self-fulfilling prophecies about what will occur.
6. If contact with others is perceived as a win-or-lose proposition, then expectations will be biased toward competition with others.
7. A third party acting as mediator might help others identify specific similarities and differences to see the other side's viewpoint more clearly.

The Cultural Grid suggests a framework of behaviors, expectations, and values on one level and social system variables on the other. (See Figure 2.1.) It is designed to facilitate accurate and appropriate expectations for multicultural contact.

This framework becomes useful in understanding an individual's personal cultural orientation to behave in expected or unexpected ways when confronted with problems. In using the grid you would first of all identify a particular behavior in yourself or someone else. Let's look at your behavior in deciding to read this book.

The second step would be to look at the expectation behind the behavior. What do you expect to happen as a result of your reading this book? Let's assume you expect to learn something you don't already know, although there are actually many different and sometimes conflicting expectations attached to a single behavior.

The third step is to identify the values on which each expectation is based. If we assume you are reading this book to learn something, then perhaps learning is an important value for you. Again, there are many different values behind each expectation, some more conscious than others.

The fourth step is to find out from where those values came. Who taught you the values that shape your expectations and direct your behavior? We may well search for the source of your values by looking at social system

Social System Variables	Behavior	Expectation	Value
Ethnographic			
nationality			
ethnicity			
religion			
language			
Demographic			
age			
gender			
affectional orientation			
physical abilities			
Status			
social			
economic			
political			
educational			
Affiliation			
formal (like family or career)			
informal (shared idea or value)			

Figure 2.1 The Intrapersonal Cultural Grid

variables. Each value, such as learning, may well come from many sources, such as family, religion, educational group, socio-economic group, ethnic or nationality background, affectional orientation, and gender group, to name but a few of the likely candidates. In any case, you know for certain that those values were taught to you by someone and did not "simply happen." The Cultural Grid is designed to help you analyze your behavior by first matching it with relevant expectations, then the values behind each expectation, and finally the social system variables that taught those values.

The Cultural Grid was introduced in a course on cross-cultural counseling where students were asked to analyze the role of culture in their interview by filling in the categories for especially significant behaviors by themselves or their culturally different client. The following excerpts provide an example from one such analysis (Fohs, 1982).

The differing social system variables are:

(1) Age. He is forty-five and I am twenty-nine. This did not seem to affect our interaction.

(2) Economic Class. He is from the lower socio-economic stratum and I am from the middle. He has experienced the feeling of no hope and I have not. Much of any difference here may be mitigated by the fact that he is now somewhat in the middle economic stratum.

(3) Affiliation. He does not perceive himself to be at all limited to his actions by his disability, at least at close quarters (he's visually disabled). This did not seem to have any effect on our interaction.

At this point in time this individual is very close to, if not already completely bicultural. To the extent that he functions effectively within his role, he has the potential of being a cultural interpreter. However, there is also the possibility that he might find himself in a position of not being completely trusted by either group if he enacts his strategy for change. I see this as a possibility, not necessarily a probability.

Many things are changing in his life right now. Because of his new job he will now be making the economic transition to the middle class. To an extent he has already started the social transition, and yet he would also like to maintain his present social network as well. His being in between may also be an issue right now as well. He gave an illustration of this indirectly when he told me about a comment by a girl client of his that she would not be able to associate with his daughters because they will be "high-classed people." This seemed to affect him quite a bit. Although he is determined not to see this happen, the fear of this possibility is in his mind.

Both behaviors and expectations are explained in a shared context. The Cultural Grid is based on the premise that culture is within the person and not within the group. The Cultural Grid was developed to identify and describe the cultural aspects of situations and to train people for culturally appropriate interaction in multicultural settings. This Cultural Grid is of course frozen in time and gives a glimpse or snapshot of how culture shapes a particular behavior only for that moment. Culture is dynamic, and the combination of variables will change from time to time, place to place, as well as from person to person.

It is difficult to locate accurately someone else's expectations and values behind their behavior, and the most a counselor can hope for is a working hypothesis or "best guess" about the expectations and values shaping a client's behavior. It is possible, however, to explore with a client the linkage between those expectations and values with his behavior. It is quite possible that unacceptable behaviors will be based on very acceptable and even honorable expectations or values. In that case it might be possible to teach the client other behaviors through which the good values and expectations might be expressed more acceptably. The Cultural Grid framework helps guide the counselor-client discussion toward integrating complex cultural variables into the counseling interview with more accurate and comprehensive understanding of the client's viewpoint.

One important implication of the Cultural Grid is that behavior is not data. Behavior can become meaningful data when that behavior is understood in the context of culturally learned expectations and values. In an attempt to understand our behaviors as culturally learned, this conceptual model provides a means to assess systematically a person's behavior according to those culturally learned expectations and values in the context of salient social-system variables. In this way, including culture in the analysis of behavior promises to increase a counselor's accuracy in understanding how similar behaviors might be the result of very different expectations and values. On the other hand, different behaviors might result from very similar expectations and values.

Culture-centered counseling is primarily focused on interpreting each behavior in its own cultural context. Approaches to counseling that ignore culture and attempt to interpret behavior independent of its culturally learned context through expectations and values are in serious danger of being inaccurate.

THE INTERPERSONAL CULTURAL GRID

The Interpersonal Cultural Grid is useful in understanding how cultural differences influence the interaction of two or more individuals. Similar behaviors may have different meanings, and different behaviors might have the same meaning as indicated in the Intrapersonal Cultural Grid. It is important to interpret behaviors accurately in terms of the expectations and values attached to those behaviors. Even if two persons are accurate in their interpretation of one another's expectations, they do not always need to display the same behavior. The two people may agree to disagree about which behavior is appropriate and continue to work together in harmony in spite of their different styles of behavior.

EXERCISE 2.2: APPLYING THE CULTURAL GRID

Identify your best friend.

Make a list of behaviors that your best friend does that are different from how you might behave in a similar situation.

Now make a list of behaviors that you do that are different from how your friend might behave in a similar situation.

What are some of the things that your best friend does to or with you that would not be acceptable if done by a stranger?

What are some of the things that you do to or with your best friend that would not be acceptable if done by a stranger?

Perhaps the expectation of best friendship the two of you share and trust provides a common ground so powerful and important that your tolerance of different behaviors is much greater than it would be for a stranger. This is an example of the Interpersonal Cultural Grid in action.

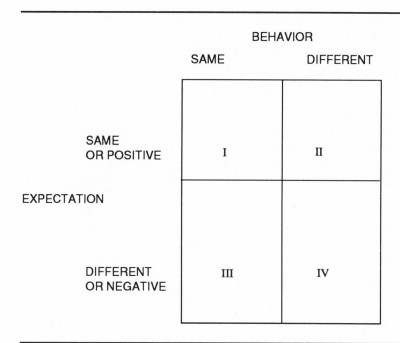

Figure 2.2 The Interpersonal Cultural Grid

Figure 2.2 divides the interaction between two individuals into four possible quadrants (Pedersen, 1988).

In the first quadrant two individuals have similar behaviors and similar positive expectations. There is a high level of accuracy in both individuals' interpretation of one another's behavior and expectations. This aspect of the relationship would be congruent and probably harmonious. We are focusing exclusively on positive expectations here. If the two individuals share the same negative expectations ("I hate you") and behavior ("I am beating you up!") the relationship may be congruent but certainly not harmonious.

In the second quadrant two individuals have different behaviors but share the same positive expectations. There is a high level of agreement that they both expect trust and friendliness, for example, but there is a low level of accuracy because each perceives and interprets the other's behavior incorrectly. This relationship is characteristic of multicultural conflict where each person is applying a self-reference criterion to interpret the other's behavior in terms of this person's own self-reference expectations and values. The conditions described in quadrant two are very unstable, and unless the shared positive expectations are quickly made explicit, the relationship is likely to change toward quadrant three.

In the third quadrant two people have the same behaviors but differ greatly in their expectations. There is actually a low level of agreement in positive expectations between the two people, even though similar or congruent behaviors give the appearance of harmony and agreement. One person may continue to expect trust and friendliness, while the other is distrustful and unfriendly, for example. Both persons are, however, presenting the same smiling behaviors.

If these two persons discover that the reason for their conflict is different expectations and if they are then able to return their relationship to an earlier stage where they did perhaps share the same positive expectations of trust and friendliness, for example, then their interaction may return to the second quadrant. This would require each to adjust his or her interpretation of the other's behavior to fit their shared positive expectation of friendship and trust. If, however, their expectations remain different, then even though their behaviors are similar and congruent, the conflict is likely to increase until their interaction moves to the fourth quadrant.

In the fourth quadrant the two people have different behaviors and also different or negative expectations. Not only do they disagree in their behaviors toward one another, but now they also disagree in their expectations of friendship and trust. This relationship is likely to result in hostile disengagement. If the two persons can be coached to increase their accuracy in identifying one another's positive expectations, however, there may still be a chance for them to return to an earlier stage of their relationship where their positive expectations were similar even though their behaviors might have been very different, as in the second quadrant.

Smiling is an ambiguous behavior. It may or may not imply trust and friendliness. The smile may or may not be interpreted accurately. Outside of its culturally learned context, the smile has no fixed meaning. Two persons with similar expectations of friendliness may not both be smiling. On the other hand, one person may expect friendliness and the other may be wanting to sell a used car, even though both of them are smiling. In a similar mode, two people may have the same expectations of trust, respect, happiness, or success, even though their culturally learned behaviors attached to the expectations may be very different.

Let us assume that you are a counselor working with a client from a different culture. You are very formal in your counseling relationships and sometimes even professionally cool. The client seems almost the opposite in style, preferring to be friendly and informal toward everyone. Now let us consider how this relationship might progress using the four quadrants of the Interpersonal Cultural Grid.

Before the counselor and client got together, they had heard good things about one another—about how the other person was friendly, trusting, respectful, and competent—so both were looking forward to working together.

This might describe the conditions of Quadrant I. The positive expectations and behaviors were congruent and similar.

During the first week the counselor and client behaved quite differently, with the client being informal and the counselor being very formal in their interactions. Each person interpreted the other's behavior negatively and contrary to the original expectation. They failed to recognize that they really shared the same expectation. Since their behaviors were so different from one another, neither one realized that they both had the same positive expectations for trust, respect, and harmony. This quadrant defines an example of cross-cultural conflict when the two persons misinterpret each other's behaviors and impose their own culturally learned interpretations.

During the second week the differences in behavior between the counselor and client have continued and are now a source of irritation and conflict between them, moving to Quadrant III. The counselor has now demanded that the client become more formal, and the client has reluctantly agreed. At this point the client no longer expects trust, respect, and harmony, however, as had been the case in Quadrants I and II, but both counselor and client are displaying the same congruent behaviors to give the appearance of harmony. Their similar behaviors might lead them and others to assume that they had the same expectations, but ultimately both counselor and client would discover the differences in expectation and probably feel betrayed.

During the third week the client is feeling very hostile at having to behave in such an unnaturally formal way, and the conflict between the counselor and client becomes more pronounced, as indicated in Quadrant IV. The client gives up and leaves counseling in order to preserve self-esteem and dignity, while the counselor willingly gives up the client also in order to preserve self-esteem and dignity. Both counselor and client will be very confused by what happened between them. The confusion is likely to result in open hostility and alienation.

The hostile disengagement of culturally different counselors and clients is not, however, inevitable. If we look at a second scenario of this hypothetical relationship, we can identify an alternative outcome. Here again is the same counselor favoring formality working with the same client who favors informality. Before getting together each has heard good things about the other and share the positive expectations and behaviors described in Quadrant I.

During the first week both the counselor and the client notice that they are behaving differently. In discussing these very different behaviors, they discover that they have the same expectations for trust, respect, and harmony, as indicated in Quadrants I and II, but that their behaviors for expressing those expectations are very different, as in Quadrant II. By calling attention to the differences in behavior and the similarity of expectations, several options are now available to them: First, they might agree to disagree about what kind of behavior is appropriate, and each person may continue with formal or informal behavior, but now the other person is better able to interpret that behavior accurately as an expression of trust and respect. Second, they might both try to bend their behavior toward the other person's preference, making an exception for that particular instance, since it is important that the shared expectation for trust and respect be communicated. Finally, by focusing on the shared common-ground expectation and not being distracted by different behaviors, the counselor and client have now established a basis for their continuing relationship without either person having to sacrifice cultural integrity by compromising values.

During the third week the counselor and client may well be bothered by the differences in behavior, although they are now able to interpret one another's behavior accurately and appropriately. They decide to concentrate on their similar positive expectations rather than on their different behaviors, and each person adjusts accordingly. Their interaction is not without conflict, but the positive shared expectations provide a common ground for them to work out differences in behavior and accommodate one another as in Quadrant II. The relationship does not move to the interpersonal conflict of Quadrants III and IV.

During the fourth week the client and counselor discover some advantages of working with a person whose behaviors are so different, as long as they can be certain of their shared positive expectations for trust, respect, and harmony as in Quadrant II.

During the fifth week the counselor and client find that they have both modified their behaviors at least with regard to one another, and now they quite often share the same behaviors as well as the same positive expectations, as in Quadrants I and II.

During the sixth week both counselor and client have learned to assess one another's behavior accurately, and the shared positive expectations for trust, harmony, and respect have been strengthened as in Quadrants I and II, contributing to the success of the counseling.

In this way the Interpersonal Cultural Grid provides a conceptual road map for the culture-centered counselor to interpret another person's behavior accurately in the context of that person's culturally learned expectations. It is not necessary for the counselor and client to share the same behaviors, as long as they share the same positive expectations.

APPLICATIONS OF THE CULTURAL GRID TO COMMUNICATION

The Cultural Grid can be a useful tool for analyzing the ways that culture influences behavior both within the person and between persons. It provides practical assistance in managing the complexity of culturally learned behaviors, expectations, and values. This combining of personal with cultural suggests a way out of a dilemma for cross-cultural research. On the one hand, there are data suggesting that cultural differences exist and must be accounted for in cross-cultural contact. On the other hand, attempts to describe cultural aspects through labels have tended to result in stereotyping. Consequently, attempts to discriminate according to cultural differences have been disguised in ways that would protect an organization or person against being accused of racism.

While the cultural label may be predictive in aggregate data about large groups from the same culture, it is less helpful in dealing with a particular individual from that culture as in a counseling situation. It is apparent that an accurate perception of another person's complex cultural perspective is an important skill for counselors in any and all situations.

Unless the cross-cultural misunderstanding or conflict is identified and distinguished from the elements of personal conflict, the following negative chain of events may occur:

1. The different behaviors will suggest that expectations may also be different.

2. As different behaviors persist, the two persons may conclude that they do not share the same expectations.

3. One of the two persons may choose to modify behaviors to match the other person, due perhaps to power constraints of the more powerful partner. However, the sense of shared expectations will become more and more divergent.

4. Both partners may ultimately resort to total conflict, where both expectations and behaviors are different and misunderstood.

5. Both partners will conclude that there is a low level of agreement between them.

6. Neither partner will be aware that there is also a low level of accuracy in their communication.

If the cross-cultural nature of the situation is identified and distinguished as separate from personal hostility, the following positive chain of events is likely to occur:

1. The different behaviors will be understood as expressions of shared positive expectations.

2. The two persons will conclude that they do share the same positive expectations, in spite of their different behaviors.

3. One or both of the two persons may choose to modify his or her behavior to match the other person's, so that both the positive expectations and the behaviors will be similar.

4. Both partners may ultimately move toward a more harmonious situation where both the positive expectations and the behaviors are similar.

5. Both partners may conclude there is either a high or a low level of agreement between them.

6. Both partners will be aware that there is a high level of accuracy in their communication.

The Cultural Grid was also used to analyze an interview transcript with a seventy-eight-year-old Irish widow and grandmother who was chronically ill and had lived in a private care facility for some years. To understand her personal cultural orientation, the counselor had to understand many factors other than age, marital status, and the nature of her illness (Pedersen and Pedersen, 1989). A content analysis of the interview emphasized the importance of independence as a strong value.

There was some conflict between her view of herself based on her extremely active and full past life and her view of herself (or perhaps her view of other people's view of herself) in the present situation. She was unwilling to give up her image as an independent and self-sufficient person in exchange for the view of herself reflected by others who described her as "aged."

Understanding her personal cultural orientation and the expectations behind her behaviors could help her counselor accurately interpret those behaviors that followed from independence and self-sufficiency among her expectations. At different points in the interview, social-system variables from different aspects of her self-identity became salient, making it difficult for the counselor to interpret her behaviors consistently from her personal cultural orientation. Each aspect of her past and present culture added a richness to the understanding of her cultural identity beyond the stereotyped description of "aged."

There is good reason to believe that counseling fulfills a need for both the counselor and the client beyond gathering information. The Cultural Grid provides structure to the culture-centered counseling interview process, suggesting criteria for evaluating both individual performance and interaction. Culturally learned values and expectations are essential data for culture-centered counseling. The Cultural Grid is a heuristic framework to help culture-centered counselors differentiate cultural from personal aspects of an interview.

EXERCISE 2.3: CASE ANALYSIS USING
THE CULTURAL GRID

A young teaching assistant goes to meet his foreign-born professor for the first time and finds him to be loud and overly friendly. In the young teaching assistant's culture, he has learned not to trust people who are so forward in their manner. The young man could see that his own contrasting quiet and submissive style was not respected by the professor, although he wanted and needed to work in harmony with him. During this initial meeting, the young man decides to become boisterous, loud, and overly friendly to reflect his professor's manner, so that they can get along with one another. Nevertheless, his first impressions of the professor are negative, and he begins to resent having to change his own ways to accommodate the professor's preferred style.

1. Describe both the young man and the professor as you see them in your mind's eye. Use at least ten adjectives, and categorize each as a demographic, ethnographic, status, or affiliation variable.

2. How do you think the professor and the young man are feeling as the young man enters the room?

3. What are some positive and negative thoughts in each of their minds?

4. What might each conclude at the end of the first meeting?

5. What cultural assumptions have influenced your own perceptions of these two people?

As an example of how the Cultural Grid might be used to analyze this complex cultural situation in Exercise 2.3, let us examine three different behaviors from this brief case study. We will work in two different directions in our analysis of them. On the one hand, we will want to consider possible alternative meanings behind the behavior and decide which meaning is more likely. On the other hand, we will want to consider the range of social-system variables inferred about the person performing the behavior and decide which is the most salient in this situation. The three behaviors are: (1) professor greets teaching assistant in a loud and overly friendly way; (2) teaching assistant responds to professor in a quiet and submissive style; (3) teaching assistant decides to become loud and boisterous toward his professor.

First, the loud and friendly greeting by the professor might express the positive expectation for friendliness grounded in the value of international harmony and learned from social systems such as his family and his previous contacts with other international students. There is the possibility of course that the professor really does not expect friendliness and is showing his superior status or is being patronizing toward foreign-born persons. Even in the midst of many negative expectations and mixed motives, it may still be possible to identify some small area of shared positive expectation. This area of common ground, however small it may be, provides the platform on which a counselor can begin to construct a meaningful and lasting relationship.

Second, the quiet and submissive greeting by the teaching assistant might express friendliness and respect grounded in the value of status and learned from social systems such as his family, religion, social group, and other sources. There also is the possibility here that the student is actually being unfriendly, apathetic, or disinterested. Here again, however, the task is to discover some small area of shared positive expectation so that the similar values can be allowed to bring the two persons closer together.

Third, the loud and boisterous adaptation by the teaching assistant might express a willingness to change his behavior in deference to the preferences of the professor as an expression of friendliness and respect grounded in values learned from social-system groups back home. The task is to go beyond the behaviors being displayed to the expectations and values behind them so that the behaviors can be interpreted accurately and appropriately.

There are several specific ways in which the Cultural Grid can be used as a practical tool for counselors.

1. The Cultural Grid provides a framework for analyzing how culturally different behaviors might derive from culturally similar expectations and values.

2. Personal-cultural orientations can be compared across time or people to demonstrate how the same behavior can be explained by different expectations or values in different cultural settings.

3. The dynamic and changing priorities of social-system variables can be matched with personal cognitive variables for each time, place, and person to prevent stereotyping.

4. A comprehensive description of culture emerges from the framework that includes demographics, status, and affiliation, as well as ethnographic variables in a broad and comprehensive range of cultural resources for each individual.

5. The close relationship between culturally learned behaviors and culturally different expectations or values behind similar behaviors combines the culturally specific "emic" with the culturally general "etic" aspects of a multicultural situation by separating areas of similarity from areas of difference.

APPLICATIONS OF THE CULTURAL GRID TO COUNSELORS

Let us consider several examples where the Cultural Grid might have a practical use in culture-centered counseling. In each of these examples, the same series of steps for applying the Cultural Grid follows. These guidelines are offered as sources of working hypotheses or "best-guess" interpretations that would be checked out with actual clients in actual counseling situations.

Step 1. Identify the relevant behaviors being displayed or presented by the person or persons.

Step 2. Identify the positive expectations that might be attached to the behavior. ("If I do this, then that will happen.")

Step 3. Identify the value variable most likely to be salient for the person or persons being considered at the time the behavior is displayed.

Step 4. Identify the social systems that may have taught the person the value upon which the expectation and ultimately the behavior are based.

Step 5. Develop rival hypotheses that put both positive and negative interpretations on the client's behavior, and consider the range of alternatives for counseling goals.

Step 6. Identify those positive expectations you think might be shared by both persons in the brief case examples as the basis of common ground in working with them.

Example 1. Your client grew up as an immigrant in a fairly rough section of New York City, but his wife grew up in a quiet rural small town. They have adopted an Indochinese refugee to live with them in New York. They argue constantly about the child. The husband encourages the child to spend time in the streets getting to know other children in the neighborhood and learning to fit in. The wife wants the child to avoid contact with other children in the neighborhood because of the dangers the child might encounter. The husband wants the child to learn the rules of the street because it is an unsafe neighborhood if you don't know the rules. The wife wants to discourage the child from spending time on the streets because it is unsafe to be there.

Common Ground. Both husband and wife have the same expectation for the safety of the child, although their behaviors are very different.

Example 2. Your client is a minority person with a handicap who doesn't work as hard as fellow employees, even though the handicap should not interfere with the person's work. How are you going to determine whether the resulting disagreements between the employee and coworkers is caused by the cultural differences between them or whether that person is manipulating the system by using cultural differences as an excuse? You would need to look beyond the behavior itself to get at the employee's expectations and values. Whether the employee does more or less work is perhaps less important than the reason why. Once you have established through contacts with the employee and other coworkers what the employee's expectations are, it should be easier to assess whether or not the employee is using cultural differences to manipulate the system.

Common Ground. Look behind the expectations and work style to find values that both the employee and coworkers share.

Example 3. You have been asked by the International Student Association to consult with the mental health clinic of a large university. They complain that all foreign students who go to the mental health clinic are diagnosed as crazy because of their different and unusual behaviors compared to American students. You work with the therapists and get across the idea that people from different cultures have appropriately different behaviors and are not necessarily crazy. A month later the International Student Association again asks you to consult with the mental health clinic because now foreign students urgently requiring therapy have been turned away, even though their behavior clearly indicated a need for psychological assistance. The therapists say that behavior of foreign students is naturally and appropriately bizarre and therapy is not required. Your task is to work with the therapists to match appropriately and accurately the range of behaviors and expectations with social-system variables.

Common Ground. Behavior is not data until and unless it is interpreted within the context of culturally learned expectations.

Example 4. Two people have come to you for help in mediating their disagreement with one another before resorting to legal action. They had grown up across the street from one another and have known one another all their lives. Their backgrounds are very similar, although one person has become increasingly more conservative and the other increasingly more liberal in their life-styles. Because they appear to one another as culturally similar, they assume that they begin with the same assumptions and any disagreement requires one of them to be wrong.

Common Ground. Cultural differences may divide persons who perceive themselves as belonging to the same culture if you define culture broadly, as these two persons do.

CONCLUSION

The practical advantage of the Cultural Grid is to increase a person's accurate assessment of another person's behavior in the context of that person's culture. Without reference to these culturally learned expectations and values, we are unable to interpret accurately any behavior outside its cultural context. The matching of cultural with personal data provides a framework for understanding how culture is related to behavior and suggests specific procedures for culture-centered counseling (Pedersen and Pedersen, 1989). In culture-centered counseling the following steps would demonstrate how the Cultural Grid can be applied.

First, identify one or more specific behaviors of an individual or conflicting behaviors among several individuals from culturally different backgrounds.

Second, try to identify the positive expectations each person or persons attach to the behavior or behaviors. What is expected to happen as a result of that behavior? There will probably be several positive expectations attached to each single behavior.

Third, try to identify the values each person or persons attach to the culturally learned positive expectation. What are the underlying values in which that positive expectation is grounded that make it important and meaningful?

Fourth, try to identify the social-system variables where those values have been taught so that you can understand the basis for the cultural values that led to expectations that led to the behavior.

In culture-centered counseling it is important not to be distracted by very different and even dissonant behaviors without first seeking out the positive expectations and values behind them. It is also important to identify the culturally learned common ground of culturally similar positive expectations and values that can then become a platform for the culture-centered counseling to begin working.

If culture is indeed within the person, then a multicultural identity becomes an essential part of each person's development. The practical advantages of the Cultural Grid are that it increases a person's accurate assessment of another person's behavior in the context of that person's culture. Without reference to these expectations and values, we are unable to interpret any behavior outside its cultural context accurately. The matching of cultural with personal data provides a framework for understanding how culture works both in the aggregate and in the individual instance. Culture-centered counselors need to go beyond the obvious labels used to describe individual and collective cultural identities. They need to recognize multicultural identity as including the synthesis of many cultures in our lives through complex and dynamic but not chaotic ways. This understanding of culture will be an important foundation for developing culture-centered counseling skills in subsequent chapters.

KEY IDEAS

1. Cultural systems define how culture works.
   Culture defines networks of people who believe similarly.
   Culture is an internalized framework or pattern.
   Cultural assumptions distinguish fact from inference.
   Culture defines similarities and differences.
2. The importance of cultural values.
   Differences between objective and subjective culture.
   Values define the boundaries of a culture.
   Values are defined by nationality, ethnicity, and role.
   Value typologies suggest a simplistic approach.
3. The Intrapersonal Cultural Grid.
   Culture is broadly defined by social-system variables.
   Personal behavior is controlled by expectations and values.
   The Cultural Grid provides a personal-cultural orientation.
   Similar behaviors may result from different expectations.

Expectations and values learned from social systems.
Unacceptable behaviors may be based on acceptable values.

4. The Interpersonal Cultural Grid.
   Cross-cultural implies similar expectations but different behaviors.
   Interpersonal implies different expectations and same or different behaviors.
   Conflict moves from the cultural to the personal quadrant.

5. Applications of the Cultural Grid.
   A tool to analyze how culture influences behavior.
   A method to prevent cultural conflict from becoming personal.
   Meaningfully separating behaviors from expectations.
   Placing behaviors in a cultural context.

6. Applications of the Cultural Grid to counseling.
   The grid suggests working hypotheses for counseling.
   Behaviors are interpreted in a cultural context.
   The focus is on culturally learned expectations.
   Expectations are interpreted by values.
   Values are rooted in social systems.
   The grid identifies the common ground of shared assumptions.

7. Conclusion.
   The Cultural Grid seeks to increase accuracy in assessment.
   The first step is to identify specific behaviors.
   Second, identify positive expectations about that behavior.
   Third, identify salient values behind expectations.
   Fourth, identify salient social systems for those values.
   Multicultural identity is the syntheses of many cultures.

EXERCISE 2.4: APPLYING THE CULTURAL GRID TO YOURSELF

Identify a friend or acquaintance with whom you have recently had an argument or disagreement. The friend or acquaintance should be someone who shares with you as many of the following characteristics as possible. Check all of those categories that are approximately the same for both of you.

Demographic: age ( ), gender ( ), neighborhood of residence ( ), affectional orientation ( ).

Ethnographic: ethnicity ( ), nationality ( ), language ( ), religion ( ).

Status: social ( ), economic ( ), educational ( ), political ( ).

Affiliations: formal ( ), informal ( ), physical issues ( ).

Cite examples of specific similarity and differences between the two of you.

Same behaviors:

Different behaviors:

Same expectations:

Different expectations:

Same values:

Different values:

How do you describe your disagreement or argument differently now than you did before analyzing that conflict using the Cultural Grid?

Chapter Three

Four Synthetic Cultures

Major Objective:
To present a four-dimensional framework of synthetic cultures as a means of understanding the importance of cultural differences for culture-centered counseling.

Secondary Objectives:
1. To define the synthetic cultures and the research on which these four dimensions is based.
2. To describe each of the four synthetic cultures in terms of their similarities and differences.
3. To apply the synthetic cultures in training culture-centered counselors.

The complexity of multiculturalism has discouraged psychological research on cultural variables. First of all, culture is not a clearly defined, universally accepted phenomenon, and there are a great many different definitions of it. Secondly, it is not always easy to differentiate between cultural and personal variables, as we demonstrated in the previous chapter. Thirdly, once you begin considering culture in a research sample, where do you stop? Do you include all values-teaching sources such as demographics, status, and affiliations, or do you arbitrarily limit yourself to ethnographic categories? Fourthly, who decides what the rules are for any given culture, and who is a legitimate interpreter of those rules? Fifthly, persons who are members of a culture may not be able to describe that culture accurately and articulately in a way that would be absolutely accepted by another person who is a member of the same culture. Because culture is so complex and dynamic, the problems of reliability and validity make it very difficult to collect data on it.

And yet, at a less abstract level, counselors working with culturally different clients and struggling with practical problems in multicultural settings demonstrate the urgency for more accurate and appropriate guidelines for multicultural counseling. Culture is obviously an important variable, even though we have not been able to measure it successfully. Culture is also an obviously important framework for sorting out the similarities and differences that unite and separate us. Culture is complex but not chaotic, and there are clearly defined patterns to be discovered. This chapter will attempt to describe four synthetic cultures as a framework to prepare counselors in culture-centered skill building, so that they will not be overwhelmed by more complex and dynamic real-world cultures.

ADVANTAGES OF SYNTHETIC CULTURES

Synthetic cultures are invented or created by synthesizing elements of many real-world cultures into extremes. Since they are extreme forms, they do not exist in the real world, although the tendency or "dimensions" demonstrated by them does exist. There are several advantages to using synthetic cultures for developing culture-centered counseling skills.

1. Because no synthetic culture replicates any particular real-world culture, it is less risky to discuss and deal with them. The consequences of conflict between synthetic cultures in a laboratory setting are less likely to violate the sensitivities of real-world cultures. If, for example, a particular culture, country, ethnic group, gender, or age group were directly discussed, any conflict or disagreement might not be as safe.

2. Because the dimension or extreme tendency demonstrated in each synthetic culture was derived from data about real-world cultures and does exist more or less in every cultural group, the learning about synthetic cultures and patterns is relevant in preparing persons to work with real-world cultures. Also, there is enough variation within each synthetic culture group of participants resulting from nationality, ethnicity, religion, age, gender, socioeconomic status, life-style, and other affiliations so that each participant's interpretation of the synthetic culture rules will be slightly different, just as in the real world.

3. Because the culture is synthetic, it is possible to control beliefs and behaviors in a less ambiguous set of rules. These synthetic culture rules are complex enough to challenge participants but not overwhelm them. The complex skills for developing awareness, knowledge, and skill are nurtured in working with synthetic cultures.

4. By teaching stereotypes, such as extreme-form synthetic cultures, it may be possible to protect people from following those stereotypes in the real world. By recognizing the extreme-form patterns in synthetic cultures, persons may be better able to recognize and deal with less extreme-form patterns among real-world cultures.

5. By deliberately assigning specific behaviors to specific expectations, participants have the opportunity to practice using the Cultural Grid and other tools of analysis and increase their facility for analyzing cultural variables to discover common ground.

6. By building the resource of the four synthetic cultures, a microcosm of cultural variability from a fifty-five–country data base is created for examining the same issue from multiple real-world viewpoints. The four synthetic cultures replicate the macrocosm of world cultures for discussing issues or topics of controversy.

7. By involving participants in four contrasting cultures, the learning becomes more personalized than an abstract discussion about cultural differences. Participants learn to articulate viewpoints from contrasting cultural perspectives.

8. By combining persons from a variety of real-world cultural backgrounds into the same synthetic culture common ground, they temporarily share one perspective. It becomes possible for people to discover other areas of real-world common ground without having to give up identities of real-world difference.

9. By temporarily taking on the new identity of a synthetic culture, people gain insights into the contrasting values of their own real-world culture. Unexamined assumptions about their own actual cultural patterns are examined and tested against the contrasting assumptions of synthetic cultures.

10. By learning the four-dimensional framework of the synthetic cultures, persons are provided with a model for organizing their experience in contrasting real-world cultures. Rather than be trained to work with a particular country or ethnic group, they are trained to identify the elements of all four synthetic cultures that present themselves in greater or lesser degrees in every new or unfamiliar cultural group.

THE EMPIRICAL BASIS OF SYNTHETIC CULTURES

The four synthetic cultures are based on research by Dr. Geert Hofstede (1980, 1986, 1991), who collected survey data about the values of people in more than fifty countries around the world. The sample for each country was drawn from the staff of IBM companies and was similar in most respects except for nationality. Hofstede therefore suggests that the differences across country samples suggest patterns of cultural difference derived from nationality.

The four dimensions that emerged from these data were: (1) small/large power distance, (2) collectivism versus individualism, (3) femininity versus masculinity, (4) weak/strong uncertainty avoidance. The labels for these constructs were used to describe patterns of similarity and difference in the distribution of responses to clusters of items across countries.

The four dimensions that emerged from these data also correspond to the three dimensions discovered earlier by Inkeles and Levinson (1969): (1) relation to authority, (2) conception of self, in particular the relationship between the individual and society and the individual's concept of masculinity and femininity, and (3) ways of dealing with conflicts, including the control of aggression and the expression of feelings (Hofstede, 1991). The distribu-

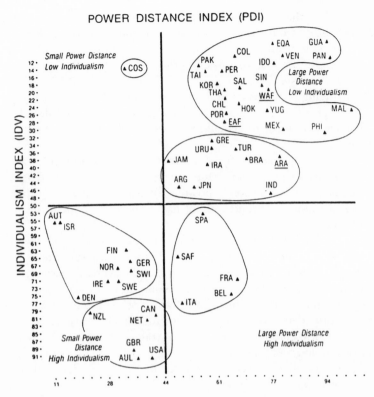

POWER DISTANCE INDEX (PDI)

Figure 3.1 A power distance × individualism—collectivism plot *for fifty countries and three regions.*

Source: Hofstede (1986): 309. By permission.

tion of country samples on the four dimensions is illustrated in Figures 3.1 and 3.2 by scattergraphs. (Table 3.1 shows the country abbreviations.)

Each synthetic culture was constructed from one end of each of Hofstede's four dimensions. In this way they were in contrast but not opposites, making it possible to find common ground between them. Each of the four will be discussed in this chapter to demonstrate the cultural patterns of belief and behavior that give that synthetic culture a cohesive identity. Beliefs and behaviors will be assigned in ways that guarantee contrasting perspectives among the four synthetic cultures and a balance of viewpoints allowing for both similarities and differences. In an earlier unpublished experiment to create synthetic cultures (Pedersen and Sprafkin, 1986), an attempt was made to incorporate multiple dimensions into each synthetic culture identity profile. However, the complexity of that approach quickly proved unmanageable and less useful than focusing on a more stereotyped, single dimension of each synthetic culture.

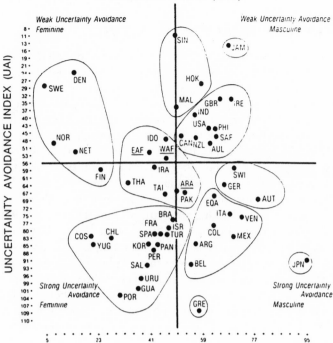

MASCULINITY INDEX (MAS)

Figure 3.2 A masculinity-femininity × uncertainty avoidance plot *for fifty countries and three regions.*

Source: Hofstede (1986): 310. By permission.

Table 3.1 Country Abbreviations

ARA Arab countries (Egypt, Lebanon, Lybia, Kuwait, Iraq, Saudi-Arabia, U.A.E.)	GER Germany	PER Peru
	GRE Greece	PHI Philippines
	GUA Guatemala	POR Portugal
	HOK Hong Kong	SAF South Africa
ARG Argentina	IDO Indonesia	SAL Salvador
AUL Australia	IND India	SIN Singapore
AUT Austria	IRA Iran	SPA Spain
BEL Belgium	IRE Ireland	SWE Sweden
BRA Brazil	ISR Israel	S̆WI Switzerland
CAN Canada	ITA Italy	TAI Taiwan
CHL Chile	JAM Jamaica	THA Thailand
COL Colombia	JPN Japan	TUR Turkey
COS Costa Rica	KOR South Korea	URU Uruguay
DEN Denmark	MAL Malaysia	USA United States
EAF East Africa (Kenya, Ethiopia, Zambia)	MEX Mexico	VEN Venezuela
	NET Netherlands	WAF West Africa
	NOR Norway	(Nigeria, Ghana,
EQA Equador	NZL New Zealand	Sierra Leone)
FIN Finland	PAK Pakistan	YUG Yugoslavia
FRA France	PAN Panama	
GBR Great Britain		

Source: Hofstede (1986): 311. By permission.

ALPHA CULTURE: HIGH POWER DISTANCE

Alpha culture accepts inequality of status and power among its members. It is accepted that some people will have more resources and opportunities than others. Inequality is seen as necessary, even justified, and undisputed. People at a lower rank are unlikely to disagree with or challenge their superiors and will prefer superiors who are autocratic or paternalistic. There is a feeling of dependence on superiors, although it might be possible for some Alphas to become "counter-dependent" and reject all authority as another form of dependency. In either case, the more powerful members of Alpha society expect and accept that power is unequally distributed.

There is a tendency for lower status and less educated Alphas to accept more authoritarian values than higher status persons (Hofstede, 1991, p. 31). One such pattern is that working-class parents are more likely to demand obedience from their children than middle-class parents. Alphas expect their children to be obedient, and there is even an order of authority among the children favoring the elder ones. Independence is discouraged, and respect for parents or other elders is encouraged. Parents and other elders reciprocate this respect with considerable warmth and caring toward children. Alpha children welcome and need or accept dependency as an important feature of healthy behavior.

In their schools Alpha teachers take on a parental role of higher power and authority, and students accept a more dependent and respectful role, especially toward older teachers. Students show their respect and deference in their behavior toward teachers, such as standing up when the teacher enters a room. Schools are teacher-centered, with the teacher organizing all communication and initiating intellectual activities. Students speak up only when allowed to do so and would never contradict or criticize a teacher even outside the school. Parents are expected to support the teacher's authority, even against their own children. Teachers are expected to transmit their personal wisdom to the students, so the quality of learning depends almost entirely on the quality of the teachers.

In their working lives, Alphas accept a hierarchical relationship and centralized power where subordinates are told what to do and not do. Alpha supervisors tend to report upward in a tall hierarchy power structure, with wide gaps in salary or rewards from the lower to the higher ranks. Lower status Alphas work harder, receive fewer privileges, and view their superiors as absolutely powerful, even when wrong. Since any anger or criticism must be internalized, Alphas often experience strong emotions they may vent against their own subordinates. The symbols of power in the workplace are visibly apparent, and subordinates take pride in their bosses' power. There is no opportunity to negotiate any disputes across power levels, and the lower ranks are expected to accept blame.

Hofstede (1991) lists some of the key characteristics of large power distance societies such as Alpha in their general norms, family, school, and workplace.

1. Inequalities are both expected and desired.
2. Less powerful people are dependent on more powerful.
3. Parents teach children to obey.
4. Children respect parents.
5. Teachers take initiatives in class.
6. Teachers transfer personal wisdom.
7. Students respect teachers.
8. Everyone values authority.
9. There is inequality between higher-ups and lower-downs.
10. Centralization is popular.
11. A wide salary range exists between the top and bottom of an organization.
12. Subordinates expect direction.
13. The boss is a benevolent autocrat or "good father."
14. Managers expect privileges.

Alphas see power as a basic fact of life more important than judgments of good or evil. The more powerful are right and legitimate by virtue of being so. The order of inequality is accepted and defines each person's place in the world, giving a sense of security to both the powerful and the powerless. The powerful are entitled to power and are expected to make use of it to their own advantage. The powerful are expected to further enhance their power whenever possible through family, friends, and force if necessary. Blame for any problems will be assigned to lower status underlings, and there is no way—except by revolution—to change the system, in which case a new power elite will emerge. Political power is managed through centralized authority, and opposition is usually limited to sporadic political violence such as occasional riots. If the power is divided it will be polarized between two powerful groups in dependent and counter-dependent alternatives. There are only a few wealthy Alphas but many poor. The laws protect the wealthy and discourage organized opposition.

Hofstede (1991) describes some key ideas of large power distance societies regarding politics and philosophy.

1. Might makes right and power is good.
2. Power and status go together.
3. The middle class is small.

4. The powerful are privileged.

5. Powerful people are impressive.

6. Power is based on the ability to control force in private and public behavior.

7. A political system is changed only by changing the people at the top (revolution).

8. Conflicts frequently lead to violence.

9. Autocratic or oligarchic governments are based on cooptation.

10. The political spectrum shows a weak center and strong wings.

11. Large income differentials in society are further increased by the tax system.

12. Religions and philosophical systems stress hierarchy and stratification.

13. Political ideologies stress power struggle.

14. Management theories focus on the appropriate role of managers.

Alphas are more likely to come from sedentary agricultural societies in more tropical areas, where they have learned to organize themselves hierarchically to keep order and balance and avoid competition with other groups. They tend to be more densely populated where power is more distant and the threat of disharmony more serious. Many Alphas come from colonized areas of the world. Alpha culture seems to be dying out and having a difficult time surviving in the modern industrialized world. However, in the postindustrialized world, as population increases and wealth become more centralized, there may be a resurgence in Alpha culture as the result of a global polarization of power.

BETA CULTURE: STRONG UNCERTAINTY AVOIDANCE

Betas have learned to cope with the high level of anxiety resulting from their strong need to avoid uncertainty in all relationships by depending on the rules of scientific technology, law, and religion. Technology helps control uncertainty in the natural world, law controls uncertainty in other people, and religion controls uncertainty in spiritual matters. The subjective and emotional impact of uncertainty is a very personal experience for Betas, and they have learned the cultural patterns necessary to avoid uncertainty wherever possible. The need to avoid uncertainty and the feeling of being threatened by the unknown is not necessarily rational, and this need may be hard for outsiders to understand. The object of anxiety is not fear of something specific but a more vaguely defined unsettling response to all uncertainty.

Betas are very expressive and talk with their hands a lot, speak loudly to show emotions, and may become "apparently" angry quite easily. They are always busy and fidgety, emotional, active, and they can become aggressive. There is a diffuse and vague feeling that anything can happen and it probably will. Betas are used to living with that ambiguity, although they don't like it. They like a lot of structure in their organizations, institutions, and relationships so that outcomes become more predictable. They might prefer a predictable but bad choice (like starting a fight in a meeting) rather than a less predictable but potentially more positive choice (like waiting to see what will happen). They drive fast and engage in Type A behavior dictated by stress and urgency. Older Betas tend to experience the most stress and require more rule orientation.

Betas have clearly defined distinctions between what is dirty and what is clean, what is dangerous and what is safe, what is good and what is bad, and they depend on clearly distinguished polarized categories to organize their lives. They tend to create rules to further distinguish good from bad. Anything different tends to be dangerous.

In their educational systems Betas expect teachers to have all the answers. Teachers who use specialized jargon are highly valued. The teacher is expected to be difficult to understand. Intellectual disagreement with the teacher will not be tolerated. At primary and secondary educational levels, parents might be brought in by a teacher but not "consulted," since the teacher is the expert.

In the workplace there are many formal and informal laws and rules to control the rights and responsibilities of both employers and employees. There are also rules for the exact work process, and these rules fill an emotional need. Nothing should be left to chance, even though some of the rules may seem unreasonable, ineffective, or inconsistent. Betas like to work hard or at least appear busy in a hurried "time-is-money" perspective. At the same time, Betas are punctual and precise in their work. Safety and security are high priorities.

Hofstede (1991) describes some key ideas of strong uncertainty avoidance cultures like Beta with regard to family, school, and workplace.

1. Life is uncertain and poses a continuous threat.

2. High stress results in a subjective feeling of anxiety.

3. Aggression and emotions may be ventilated at proper times and places.

4. Acceptance of familiar risks is not the same as fear of ambiguous situations and unfamiliar risks.

5. Tight rules are applied to children on what is dirty or taboo.

6. What is different is dangerous.

7. Students are comfortable in structured learning situations and concerned with the right answers.

8. Teachers have all the answers.
9. There is an emotional need for rules, even if they will never work.
10. Time is money.
11. There is an emotional need to be busy and an inner urge to work hard.
12. Precision and punctuality come naturally.
13. There is a suppression of deviant ideas or behavior and a resistance to innovation.
14. They are motivated by security and esteem or the feeling of belonging.

In their political relationships Betas are guided by precise written and comprehensive laws and/or rules that govern behavior. Power differences are less important than differences in competence. Betas tend to be pessimistic about influencing the decision of authorities, and they are unlikely to protest decisions. They may tolerate demonstrations or petitions but believe that more extreme protests should be repressed by the government. Betas feel they are dependent on the expertise of authorities and protect the status quo of the establishment. They tend to be politically conservative and favor law-and-order priorities. Betas are expected to carry proof of their identity and show that proof on demand. There is always the danger of extremist or even terrorist minorities among Betas, whose ideas and actions must be banned. Betas tend to be xenophobic and chauvinistic toward others. Fascism and racism are popular among Betas. There is a tendency to avoid and deny conflict while repressing or assimilating the minorities causing this conflict. The potential for conflict is high.

Religious beliefs are important to Betas for reducing ambiguity. They tend to prefer Western religions that accept the notion of Absolute Truth, with its emphasis on salvation and conversion, rather than the more encompassing Eastern religions. The same principle applies to philosophical and social ideologies, where those ideas favoring absolute truths and "grand theories" are favored. It is difficult to maintain friendships if parties have different beliefs.

Hofstede (1991) describes key ideas among strong uncertainty avoidance societies such as Betas.

1. There are many precise laws and rules.
2. Rules must be respected.
3. Citizen incompetence is a challenge to authority.
4. Citizen protest is repressed.
5. Citizens are negative toward institutions.
6. Civil servants are negative toward the political process.

7. Conservatism, extremism, law, and order are popular.

8. They have negative attitudes toward young people.

9. Nationalism, xenophobia, and repression of minorities are accepted.

10. There is a belief in experts and specialization.

11. There are many doctors but few nurses.

12. There is only one Truth.

13. They believe in religious, political, and ideological fundamentalism and intolerance.

14. In philosophy and science there is a tendency toward "grand theories."

15. Scientific opponents cannot be personal friends.

Betas are often wealthier than their neighbors, and their history is rooted in powerful centralized states governed by laws. They tend to become more prominent during times of high stress associated with the danger of war. As anxiety increases, Beta emphasis on fundamentalism and xenophobia becomes more popular.

GAMMA CULTURE: HIGH INDIVIDUALISM

Most of the world's populations do not believe in individualism as do Gammas, making Gamma a more exotic culture in numerical terms. For Gammas, the interests of individuals are more important than those of the groups to which they belong. They live in nuclear families with little attention to extended ties. They define themselves according to individual characteristics and see independence as an important goal. It would be disadvantageous to become dependent on any group for anything. There are loose ties to other individuals, but all are expected to take care of themselves. Personal time, freedom, and challenge are important to Gammas. Gammas are frequently wealthy and pride themselves on their individual achievements of accumulating that wealth. They like to say what they think, irrespective of the consequences, as a mark of their honesty and sincerity. Confrontation and debate will quickly sort out who is right and who is wrong. Others need to learn how to accept direct feedback without being offended. Gammas talk a lot and feel obligated to avoid silence in groups.

Gamma children tell the truth as they see it and learn early to cope with conflict. They develop their own opinions, unless they are inferior or weak, and get jobs to earn their own spending money. Students are expected to speak up in class and will compete with one another for attention. If the teacher shows favoritism toward a special student, it will be judged unfair by the other students. Students expect to be judged individually and impartially, without regard to the groups to which they belong. The whole purpose of education is personal advancement and to learn skills that will help advancement in the future. Certificates and diplomas are symbols of individual accomplishment providing a sense of worth and self-respect.

In the workplace Gammas also act in their own self-interest which, hopefully, will coincide with that of the employer. Gammas would not use family relationships to help them advance at work and would judge this as unfair nepotism. The relationship between employer and employee is a practical business contract between a buyer and a seller, and that contract can be broken by either party when a better one becomes available. Employees are moved around with incentives and bonuses linked to their individual performance. Management techniques and training are emphasized by Gammas, such as conducting performance appraisal interviews or management by objectives. A good manager knows how to give an employee bad news. Sensitivity training is popular where conflicts are discussed openly by Gammas and where there is an open and direct exchange of feelings. The task is always more important than relationships.

Hofstede (1991) presents key ideas of highly individualist Gamma cultures with regard to family, school, and the workplace.

1. Look after your immediate (nuclear) family.
2. Identity is an individual possession.
3. Children think in terms of "I."
4. Honest persons speak their mind.
5. Low-context communication (abstract concepts) is preferred.
6. Trespassing leads to guilt and loss of self-respect.
7. The purpose of education is learning how to learn.
8. Diplomas increase one's economic worth and/or self-respect.
9. The relationship between employer and employee is a contract based on mutual advantage.
10. Hiring and promotion decisions are based on skills and rules.
11. Management is the management of individuals.
12. The task prevails over relationships.

Gammas consider individualism to be superior to alternative perspectives. They believe their individualism is the reason for their wealth and superior political power in the world as well as the foundation of their national greatness. In their economic relationships they believe that self-interest is the best guide for determining fair economic values. Economic theories supporting and defending individualism are popular among Gammas but quite often do not work as well in other cultures. Self-actualization is an important psychological construct for Gammas, and "doing your own thing" is a natural right.

Hofstede (1991) describes some of the key ideas of individualistic societies like Gamma with regard to politics and ideas.

1. Individuals prevail over collective interests.
2. Everyone values privacy.
3. Everyone has a private opinion on any topic.
4. Laws and rights are the same for all.
5. They expect to have a higher per capita GNP than others.
6. There is a restrained role of the state in the economic system.
7. Their economy is based on individual interests.
8. Political power is exercised by voters.
9. There is press freedom.
10. Native economic theories are based on the pursuit of individual self-interests.
11. Individual freedom prevails over the need for equality.
12. Self-actualization is an ultimate goal.

Gammas believe the future belongs to them because they will control the wealth. They also believe that when a country's wealth increases, citizens become more individualistic in guarding their own resources and less dependent on others. Gammas come from countries with moderate and cold climates and are more individualistic because survival depends more on personal initiative. They believe in population control and promote small families to conserve their limited resources; they are frequently in conflict with more collectivist cultures where population growth is less controlled. Gammas believe they have an obligation to teach everyone else to become more like themselves.

DELTA CULTURE: HIGHLY MASCULINE

Deltas take great interest in achievements, assertiveness, competitiveness, and being "tough." Social gender roles are distinctly separated, with women being more modest, tender, and concerned with the quality of life, although even the women admire and respect the men for their superior status and will model their behavior more after Delta men than might women in other cultures. The men dominate politics, the community, and the workplace.

In the Deltas' upbringing, both boys and girls learn to be ambitious and competitive, with the girls supporting the boys in their achievements. Girls are cheerleaders and boys play football. Strong, popular male heroes are admired by both boys and girls. Delta students are visible in class and compete openly with one another. Failing in school would be a disaster for

Deltas, for whom performance is very important. Deltas value teachers who are brilliant and have a strong academic reputation. Men teach at the university levels with high status, and women tend to teach younger children in positions of lower status.

In the workplace Deltas tend to be assertive, rather than modest, toward others. Conflicts are resolved directly and "may the best man win." Deltas value success on the job and live in order to work; others might call Deltas workaholics. They stress results and will reward those who perform well. Delta men are expected to have high aspirations for career advancement, although this would be less important among Delta women, who would share in their men's success. Delta women who are successful take on many male characteristics in their own life-styles. Deltas require a lot of recognition for their accomplishments, opportunities to advance themselves, and challenges against which they can test their ability. A good boss is assertive, decisive, and aggressive. He makes his own decisions based on the facts, and he will be expected to be somewhat "macho." Deltas are proud of their industrial advantage in manufacturing, efficiency, and productivity and use related data to demonstrate the superiority of the Delta perspective.

Hofstede (1991) describes key ideas of masculine societies such as Delta with regard to the family, school, and workplace.

1. Material success and progress are dominant values.
2. Money and material things are important.
3. Men are assertive, ambitious, and "tough."
4. Woman are tender and take care of relationships.
5. Fathers deal with facts, and mothers with feelings.
6. Boys don't cry but fight back when attacked; girls don't fight but cry.
7. There is sympathy for the strong.
8. The best student sets the norm.
9. Failing is a disaster.
10. Brilliance in teachers is appreciated.
11. Boys and girls study different subjects.
12. They live in order to work.
13. Managers are expected to be decisive and assertive.
14. There is much stress on equity and competition among colleagues.
15. Conflicts are resolved by fighting them out.

In their political perspectives, Deltas value performance and criticize weakness. Taxes are resented by Deltas as holding back the successful and wealthy while subsidizing weaker, unsuccessful people. Deltas are not tolerant of crime, drugs, bribery, prostitution, divorce, or suicide. Deltas appreciate largeness; "big is beautiful." Deltas give priority to growth and development, even at the sacrifice of the environment. The arms race between two Delta countries becomes a contest of strength.

Deltas are not embarrassed about their unequal treatment of women, and many Deltas will quote the Bible to demonstrate the rightness of their male-dominated perspective. Deltas believe God is a man.

Hofstede (1991) describes the key ideas of masculine societies like Deltas with regard to politics and ideas.

1. Good performance is an ideal of society.

2. Strong people should be supported.

3. Society should be corrective.

4. Bigger and faster are better.

5. The maintenance of economic growth has highest priority.

6. The government should spend a relatively small proportion of its budget on assistance to poor countries.

7. The government should spend a relatively large proportion of its budget on armaments.

8. International conflicts are resolved by a show of strength or by fighting.

9. There are few women in elected political positions.

10. Religions stress the male prerogative.

11. Women seek admission to positions hitherto only occupied by men.

With regard to future trends, there seems to be a polarization of Deltas and their opposites in the world, with fewer and fewer cultures being moderate. Populations with a younger average age tend to favor Delta culture, especially among young men, while older populations do not agree with Deltas. With increased population control and higher average age in many countries, Deltas may have a more difficult time in the future. The increased power and liberation of women in many cultures will also be difficult for Deltas. Finally, the emphasis on ecological conservation is also contrary to basic Delta values.

A SYNTHETIC CULTURE TRAINING DESIGN

The four synthetic cultures, Alpha, Beta, Gamma, and Delta, represent four extreme-form contrasting perspectives that are present in all cultures in various degrees depending on the culture itself, the time, place, and situation. Becoming familiar with these four synthetic cultures should make it possible to identify similarities and differences across cultures. While a particular culture may emphasize one of these dimensions more than another—as indicated in the scattergraphs provided by Hofstede from his data—in the individual case a person from that culture may present a very different profile. The framework provided by the four synthetic cultures prepares a person to adapt to individual variations in each unfamiliar culture by increasing the repertoire of appropriate responses.

There are several ways that the synthetic cultures can be used in training. One that has proven successful is to structure their interaction with one another as four host cultures from each of the synthetic cultures interacting with four teams of visiting consultants from each of the synthetic cultures. The objectives of this training design are to:

1. Teach the four contrasting cultural perspectives identified by Hofstede in his data.

2. Establish a common ground among culturally different participants as they interpret their shared synthetic culture differently.

3. Identify similarities and differences between each participant's real culture and the assumed synthetic culture identity.

4. Learn to provide help to culturally different people without abandoning (synthetic) cultural integrity.

The training design will be described in a series of activities to be followed in sequence. A brief set of assigned beliefs and behaviors for each synthetic culture will also be provided.

The first step is to assemble a group of persons as small as sixteen, with four persons to each synthetic culture group, or as large as about fifty, with the four synthetic cultures varying in size but with none being smaller than four persons. The participants may be assigned purposely to a particular synthetic culture for whatever reason, or they may be allowed to choose one culture after a brief presentation of all to the group. When participants choose a synthetic culture it may be because it is very close to their home culture, or it may be very unfamiliar. The simulation seems to work better when participants select, for whatever reason, a synthetic culture for themselves. If participants are going to be allowed to select synthetic cultures, then the brief set of assigned beliefs and behaviors for each should be read to the entire group beforehand so that there is a basis for making a selection. If participants are to be assigned to a particular synthetic culture, you may not want them to have advance knowledge about any synthetic culture other than their own. The simulation seems to work best, however, when all participants know as much as they want about all four synthetic cultures.

The second step is to distribute the guidelines indicating beliefs and behaviors of each synthetic culture to those persons in it. If the simulation is run with open access, then each participant will be given the rules for all four synthetic cultures. If the simulation is run with closed access, then participants will be given only those rules for their own synthetic culture. In the past open access has seemed to result in the most learning.

The third step is to instruct each group to socialize within their new synthetic culture. They will do this by reading over the guidelines. Ideally, the participants will already have read over the description of each synthetic culture earlier in this chapter. As the participants read about their new culture, they will be expected to ask questions and interact with one another using the beliefs and behaviors of their synthetic culture. Usually thirty minutes is sufficient for participants to learn the beliefs and behaviors.

The fourth step is to have participants identify the problems that have resulted from "outsiders" coming into their synthetic culture community. Those other cultures may be the other three synthetic cultures or some other culture or cultures, depending on the specific goals of the workshop. Each synthetic culture group should be able to identify at least ten negative effects of this migration of outsiders into their community. The consulting teams which will be sent out from each synthetic culture to each other synthetic culture will attempt to help the host culture deal with these problems. This discussion may be included as part of the third step orientation/socialization process, or it may require an additional ten minutes.

The fifth step is to select a team of two or more consultants from each synthetic culture who will be sent to one of the other synthetic cultures to help them solve the problem of outsiders. There will be three opportunities to send out consultant teams, so the teams may either be the same two or more persons or different consultants. The selection of consultants may be included as part of steps three and four, or it may require an additional five minutes.

The sixth step is for each synthetic culture to send its team of consultants to another host culture. In the first round the Alpha team may be sent to Beta culture, the Beta team to Gamma culture, and so on. The consultant teams will be allowed from ten to fifteen minutes to help the host culture solve the problems of outsiders. The team of consultants and the host culture persons are instructed to stay in their synthetic culture roles during the consultation. At the end of the ten or fifteen minutes, all participants are instructed to go out of role and discuss the interaction. What worked and what did not work, and why? What did they learn about the synthetic cultures, about each other, and about themselves that might be useful in working with real-world cultures? After debriefing one another for five or ten minutes, each consultant team is sent back to its original synthetic culture to report what was learned.

The seventh step is for the consultant teams to report to the home culture what they learned, and the home culture to report on what it learned from the consultant team's visit. After about ten minutes of debriefing, each synthetic culture is instructed to prepare consultants for a visit to another host culture. The sixth and seventh steps are now repeated with the two other cultures.

The eighth step is for each synthetic culture to report back to the larger group on (1) what they learned about their own synthetic culture; (2) what they learned about the other three synthetic cultures; and (3) what they learned about themselves, which might be helpful in working with real-world cultures. Each group should be allowed five to ten minutes to report.

The ninth step is a debriefing of the workshop by the workshop leader, pointing out some of the cultural patterns discussed earlier in this book as well as other insights from observing the teams in action.

When the workshop group includes fewer than sixteen participants, it is useful to put all the members of one group with all the members of another group, rather than send out consultants. In the first round all Alphas would meet with all Betas and all Gammas with all Deltas, and so on. The entire group would spend ten minutes role-playing a negotiation/mediation session, followed by ten minutes out of role discussing what they learned and another ten minutes with each synthetic culture withdrawing to discuss strategies for the next round and consolidate learning.

Once a class or workshop group has become familiar with its own synthetic culture, it is possible to set up a variety of situations for training culture-centered counselors. Some of these possibilities might include:

1. Assign counselors from a synthetic culture to work with clients from a contrasting synthetic culture in a brief interview—either one-on-one or in a group setting.

2. Develop a group including persons from all four synthetic cultures and role-play a group counseling experience.

3. Assign counselors who are not familiar with the four synthetic cultures to role-play a group or individual counseling interview with clients from the synthetic cultures.

4. Assign a series of counselors from each synthetic culture to work with the same clients on the same problems to see how their approaches might be different.

5. Discuss the same problem in the four separate synthetic culture groups to identify an appropriate approach for dealing with that problem, and then report that finding to the larger group.

6. Discuss a problem in the larger group with participants from the four synthetic cultures responding in role to one another during the discussion.

7. Apply the Triad Model (Pedersen, 1988), matching a three-person team from the same synthetic culture—one as a coached client, one as an

anti-counselor, and one as a pro-counselor—to work with a counselor for a ten-minute interview.

8. Videotape any of the above exercises and debrief the group by discussing it.

The participants and facilitators may well come up with other variations using the four synthetic cultures as a safe way to develop working with more complex and dynamic real-world cultures on real problems. In any case, it will be important to have clearly specified objectives ahead of time, and it will be important to evaluate the exercise afterward to see if it accomplished those objectives or not.

SYNTHETIC CULTURE BELIEFS AND BEHAVIOR GUIDELINES

The following guidelines will help facilitators guide participants to simulate the four synthetic cultures.

Alpha Culture (High Power Distance)

Power distance indicates the extent to which a culture accepts that power is unequally distributed in institutions and organizations.

Alpha Behaviors

I. Language
   A. Alphas will use the following words with a *positive* meaning: respect, father (as a title), master, servant, older brother, younger brother, wisdom, favor, protect, obey, orders, pleasing.
   B. Alphas will use the following words with a *negative* meaning: rights, complain, negotiate, fairness, task, necessity, codetermination, objectives, question, criticize.
II. The Cultural Grid
   A. The following behaviors will express the following expectations in Alpha culture.

Behavior	Expectation
Soft-spoken, polite, listening	Friendly
Quiet, polite, not listening	Unfriendly
Ask for help and direction	Trust
Do not ask for help and direction	Distrust
Passive, but no eye contact	Interest
Expressionless, unanimated, but with eye contact	Boredom

III. Barriers
  A. Language: Alphas are very verbal but usually soft spoken and polite.
  B. Nonverbal: Alphas are usually restrained and formal.
  C. Stereotypes: Alphas are hierarchical and seek to please.
  D. Evaluation: Alphas tend to blame themselves for any problems that come up.
  E. Stress: Alphas internalize stress and express it indirectly.

Beta Culture (Strong Uncertainty Avoidance)

Uncertainty avoidance indicates the lack of tolerance in a culture for uncertainty and ambiguity.

Beta Behaviors

  I. Language
  A. Betas will use the following words with a *positive* meaning: structure, duty, truth, law, order, certain, clear, clean, secure, safe, predictable, tight.
  B. Betas will use the following words with a *negative* meaning: maybe, creative conflict, tolerant, experiment, spontaneous, relativity, insight, unstructured, loose, flexible.
  II. The Cultural Grid
  A. The following behaviors by Betas will indicate the following expectations.

Behavior	Expectation
Detailed responses, formal and unambiguous, specific	Friendly
Generalized, ambiguous responses, anxious to end the interview	Unfriendly
Polarized responses separate right from wrong unambiguously	Trust
Openly critical and challenging the other person's credentials	Distrust
Verbal and active questioning with direct eye contact, task oriented	Interest
Passive and quiet with no direct eye contact	Boredom

III. Barriers
  A. Language: Betas are very verbal and well organized, somewhat loud.
  B. Nonverbal: Betas are animated in using hands but with little or no physical contact.
  C. Stereotypes: Betas have rigid beliefs that don't change easily.

D.   Evaluation: Betas quickly evaluate a situation to establish right and wrong, sometimes prematurely.

E.   Stress: Betas externalize stress and usually make the other person feel it.

Gamma Culture (High Individualism)

Individualism indicates the extent to which a culture believes that people are supposed to take care of themselves and remain emotionally independent of groups, organizations, and other collectivities.

Gamma Behaviors

I.   Language

A.   Gammas will use the following words with a *positive* meaning: self, friendship, do your own thing, contract, litigation, self-respect, self-interest, self-actualizing, individual, dignity, I/me, pleasure, adventurous, guilt.

B.   Gammas will use the following words with a *negative* meaning: harmony, face, we, obligation, sacrifice, family, tradition, decency, honor, duty, loyalty, shame.

II. The Cultural Grid

A.   Gammas will display the following behaviors when they intend the following expectations.

Behavior	Expectation
Verbal and self-disclosing	Friendly
Criticize other persons behind their backs, sabotage enemies	Unfriendly
Aggressively debate issues and control an interview actively	Trust
Noncommittal on issues and more passive, ambiguous, or defensive	Distrust
Loudly verbal with lots of questions, touching, and close physical contact	Interest
Maintain physical distance with no questions or eye contact	Boredom

III. Barriers

A.   Language: Gammas are verbal and self-centered, using "I" and "me" a lot.

B.   Nonverbal: Gammas touch a lot and are somewhat seductive.

C.   Stereotypes: Gammas are defensive and tend to be loners who see others as potential enemies.

D.   Evaluation: Gammas use other people and measure the importance of others in terms of how useful they are.

E. Stress: Gammas like to take risks and like the challenge of danger to test their own ability.

Delta Culture (Highly Masculine)

Masculinity indicates the extent to which traditional masculine values of assertiveness, money, and things prevail in a culture as contrasted to traditional feminine values of nurturance, quality of life, and people.

Delta Behaviors

I. Language

  A. Deltas will use the following words with a *positive* meaning: career, competition, fight, aggressive, assertive, success, winner, deserve, merit, balls, excel, force, big, hard, fast, quantity.

  B. Deltas will use the following words with a *negative* meaning: quality, caring, solidarity, modesty, compromise, help, love, grow, small, soft, slow, tender.

II. The Cultural Grid

  A. Deltas display the following behaviors when they intend the following expectations.

Behavior	Expectation
Physical contact, seductive and loud	Friendly
Physical distance, sarcastic and sadistic	Unfriendly
Tend to dominate discussion and be competitive	Trust
Openly critical, disparaging, and attempt to end the discussion	Distrust
Sports oriented and eager to debate every issue from all points of view	Interest
No eye contact, discourteous, drowsy	Boredom

III. Barriers

  A. Language: Deltas are loud and verbal with a tendency to criticize and argue with others.

  B. Nonverbal: Deltas like physical contact, direct eye contact, and animated gestures.

  C. Stereotypes: Deltas are macho, hero and status oriented, and like winners.

  D. Evaluation: Deltas are hard to please, tend to be overachievers, defensive, and blame others for their mistakes.

  E. Stress: Deltas are Type A personalities, generating stress through fast-paced life-styles.

It is important to generalize from the four synthetic cultures to real-world cultures. The synthetic cultures are useful to demonstrate how real-world cultures contrast with one another in emphasis but also to demonstrate that they each combine aspects of every synthetic culture to some extent. To demonstrate your ability to generalize from the synthetic cultures to a more complex real world, identify specific aspects of the four synthetic cultures that you have experienced in your contact with the following real-world cultures.

Identify a particular example of a real world culture that belongs to one of the following categories and indicate which aspects of the four synthetic cultures you associate with that particular group based on your own experience.

Real World Cultural Category	Salient Synthetic Culture

   I. Ethnographic
      A. Nationality
      B. Ethnic groups (African-American, Asian-
         American, Hispanic, Native American,
         other)
      C. Religious group
      D. Language group
  II. Demographic
      A. Gender group
      B. Age group
      C. Place of residence group
 III. Status groups
      A. Social
      B. Economic
      C. Educational
 IV. Affiliations
      A. Formal (family, job, etc.)
      B. Informal (idea, value, etc.)

KEY IDEAS

1.   The advantages of synthetic culture.
      Synthetic cultures provide a safe context for training.
      Extreme examples help identify contrasting alternatives.
      Synthetic cultures can be defined and controlled.
      Familiarity with stereotypes may facilitate analysis.
      Specific behaviors can be linked to specific expectations.
      Synthetic cultures are based on empirical data.
      Cultural contrasts become more personalized in roles.
      Synthetic culture groups combine real culture differences.

Synthetic alternatives help clarify real culture beliefs.
The synthetic culture framework is convenient for analysis.

2. The empirical basis of synthetic cultures.
    Synthetic cultures based on Hofstede's four dimensions.
    Hofstede's research based on a fifty-five–country sample.

3. Alpha culture based on high power distance.
    Inequality of status and power is accepted.
    More authoritarian values are applied.
    Hierarchical relationships are preferred.

4. Beta culture based on strong uncertainty avoidance.
    A need to avoid uncertainty and ambiguity in relationships.
    Clear structure is preferred for all tasks.
    Laws and rules are important.

5. Gamma culture based on high individualism.
    Individuals are more important than groups.
    Competitive in their relationships.
    Self-interest is of primary concern.

6. Delta culture based on high masculinity.
    Achievement and assertiveness are important.
    Male roles are dominant over female roles.
    Sports oriented in their metaphors.

7. A synthetic culture training design.
    Groups are divided into four synthetic subgroups.
    Each synthetic subgroup learns cultural rules.
    Synthetic subgroups send out consultants to seek common ground.
    Debrief on strategies to bridge cultural differences.
    Alternative ways to use synthetic cultures in training.

EXERCISE 3.1: SELF-AWARENESS INVENTORY

Put an "X" at the appropriate number on the following scales to indicate your own perspective and your perception of the perspectives taken by each of the four synthetic cultures.

1. A person's identity lies within . . .
    the individual 1 2 3 4 5 6 7   the family
    Yourself
    Alpha
    Beta
    Gamma
    Delta

2. A person should place reliance on . . .
                  others   1   2   3   4   5   6   7   self
        Yourself
        Alpha
        Beta
        Gamma
        Delta

3. A person learns from . . .
                  personal   1   2   3   4   5   6   7   the wisdom of others
                  experience
        Yourself
        Alpha
        Beta
        Gamma
        Delta

4. I am motivated by the need to . . .
                  improve self   1   2   3   4   5   6   7   be liked
        Yourself
        Alpha
        Beta
        Gamma
        Delta

5. I view other people's motives as . . .
                  suspicious   1   2   3   4   5   6   7   basically trustful
        Yourself
        Alpha
        Beta
        Gamma
        Delta

6. I define friendship as including . . .
                  many people   1   2   3   4   5   6   7   few people
        Yourself
        Alpha
        Beta
        Gamma
        Delta

7. In a social situation I feel that friendly aggression (teasing, one-upmanship, etc.)
    is . . .
        acceptable and fun   1   2   3   4   5   6   7   embarrassing
        Yourself
        Alpha
        Beta
        Gamma
        Delta

8. I deal with conflict . . .

                    directly 1 2 3 4 5 6 7   indirectly through others
        Yourself
        Alpha
        Beta
        Gamma
        Delta

9. I approach activity with a concern for . . .

                 doing things 1 2 3 4 5 6 7   being together
                     together
        Yourself
        Alpha
        Beta
        Gamma
        Delta

10. My usual pace of life is . . .

                   fast, busy 1 2 3 4 5 6 7   slow, relaxed
        Yourself
        Alpha
        Beta
        Gamma
        Delta

11. I solve problems by . . .

          goal-based analysis 1 2 3 4 5 6 7   past knowledge or
                                                      experience
        Yourself
        Alpha
        Beta
        Gamma
        Delta

12. I define time in terms of the . . .

                       future 1 2 3 4 5 6 7   past
        Yourself
        Alpha
        Beta
        Gamma
        Delta

13. Nature is . . .

                 mystical and 1 2 3 4 5 6 7   physical and knowledgeable
                       fateful
        Yourself
        Alpha
        Beta
        Gamma
        Delta

14. I am generally . . .
    very clean 1 2 3 4 5 6 7 indifferent to cleanliness
    Yourself
    Alpha
    Beta
    Gamma
    Delta

15. I feel ultimately that what is desired can be achieved . . .
    if one works hard 1 2 3 4 5 6 7 in very limited measure
    Yourself
    Alpha
    Beta
    Gamma
    Delta

16. Youth should . . .
    show deference to 1 2 3 4 5 6 7 lead progress in the
    wiser elders   country
    Yourself
    Alpha
    Beta
    Gamma
    Delta

17. Feelings should be . . .
    suppressed 1 2 3 4 5 6 7 freely expressed
    Yourself
    Alpha
    Beta
    Gamma
    Delta

18. Personal beliefs should . . .
    conform 1 2 3 4 5 6 7 be asserted
    Yourself
    Alpha
    Beta
    Gamma
    Delta

19. In your life direction you should . . .
    follow a self- 1 2 3 4 5 6 7 do what is needed of you
    determined course
    Yourself
    Alpha
    Beta
    Gamma
    Delta

20. Problem solving should be . . .
        deliberated and 1 2 3 4 5 6 7   instinctive and impulsive
             logical
    Yourself
    Alpha
    Beta
    Gamma
    Delta

21. Manual labor is good for . . .
        the lower classes 1 2 3 4 5 6 7   anyone
    Yourself
    Alpha
    Beta
    Gamma
    Delta

22. The best way to learn is . . .
        by mistakes 1 2 3 4 5 6 7   from others
    Yourself
    Alpha
    Beta
    Gamma
    Delta

23. Change . . .
        is possible 1 2 3 4 5 6 7   happens by chance effort
    Yourself
    Alpha
    Beta
    Gamma
    Delta

24. With regard to the family . . .
        other relationships 1 2 3 4 5 6 7   there is a strong
        are valued as more   relationship and loyalty
             important
    Yourself
    Alpha
    Beta
    Gamma
    Delta

25. For the underdog, there is a feeling of . . .
        empathy 1 2 3 4 5 6 7   scorn
    Yourself
    Alpha
    Beta
    Gamma
    Delta

26. Authority is . . .

     resented and   1 2 3 4 5 6 7   respected and valued
     rebelled against
     Yourself
     Alpha
     Beta
     Gamma
     Delta

27. Inefficiency and red tape . . .

     are unimportant 1 2 3 4 5 6 7   can't be tolerated
     Yourself
     Alpha
     Beta
     Gamma
     Delta

28. The style of communication is . . .

     tactful, indirect 1 2 3 4 5 6 7   open, direct
     Yourself
     Alpha
     Beta
     Gamma
     Delta

29. Elders receive . . .

     respect and 1 2 3 4 5 6 7   disrespect and disregard
     deference
     Yourself
     Alpha
     Beta
     Gamma
     Delta

30. Concerning technology, it . . .

     is the foundation 1 2 3 4 5 6 7   needs control
     for progress in the
     future
     Yourself
     Alpha
     Beta
     Gamma
     Delta

Part Two

Culture-Centered Skill Development

Culture-centered counseling skills build on appropriate awareness and accurate knowledge about one's own culture and the contrasting cultures around us. Culture-centered skills are sensitive to contextual variables of ethnography (nationality, ethnicity, religion, language), demography (age, gender, affectional orientation, place of residence), status (social, educational, economic), affiliations (formal and informal), counselor's behaviors and style, counselor's expectations and values, and the organizational setting. The pattern of these complex and dynamic factors is what we call culture and is the focus of culture-centered counseling. The culture-centered approach is also based on social skills training.

Carl Rogers (Kurtz and Marshall, 1982) developed practical skills that facilitate the helping relationship by demystifying it and streamlining the training of counselors. Because of him counselor training focused on helper attitudes and developing a facilitative context. In addition to didactic training a new emphasis on experiential training became popular where attitudes as well as facts were taught. This experiential approach helped students discriminate between facilitative and non-facilitative therapy through recorded and live demonstrations, role-playing, participating in group or individual therapy, and receiving supervision on interviews. With this new open and practical approach to training, counseling went public.

Truax and Carkhuff (1967) developed a didactic-experiential model integrating the training environment with facilitative supervision, didactic training to discriminate among core conditions of counseling, and a group experience to explore the counselor trainee's own changing attitudes. This approach led to Carkhuff's systematic human relations training model. Other counselor educators borrowed from skill training as well. Kagan developed a model for "interpersonal process recall" using video in training, while Danish and Hauer developed a "helping skills program" in this new approach to skill training (Kurtz and Marshall, 1982).

Ivey (Ivey and Authier, 1978; Baker and Daniels, 1989) developed the microcounseling model of combining a conceptual framework with core helping skills that discriminate among the discrete behaviors that define good counseling. This changed the focus from helper attitudes and qualities to operational techniques and behaviors, as well as from person- or trainee-centered training to skills-centered training. These skills can be learned and incorporated into the counselor's style.

The skills training approach used in this book is that of microcounseling (Ivey, 1971; Ivey and Authier, 1978; Ivey, 1988), which focuses on discrete behaviors that define good counseling. Over the years microcounseling has become the most researched form of skills training, with over 250 studies attesting to its validity (Baker and Daniels, 1989; Baker, Daniels, and Greeley, 1990; Daniels, 1985; Ivey and Authier, 1978). Furthermore the model has been used widely throughout the world and has been translated into at least fourteen languages. Settings for microskill training have included many culturally varied populations, including Japanese and German managers, Australian aboriginal social workers, UNESCO AIDS education officials, and Puerto Rican volunteer peer helpers.

Microcounseling was one of the first skills training approaches to point out the need for adapting skills training to multicultural settings. Nwachuku and Ivey (1991) suggest the following steps for generating culturally relevant theory and practice.

1. Examine the culture itself. What are important personal and interpersonal characteristics in this culture?
2. Identify concrete skills and strategies that can be used in modern helping relationships. Organize these strategies into patterns and test them in practice.
3. Test the new helping theory and its skills in action.

In the application of culture-centered counseling skills, it will be important to apply these steps to test the accuracy and appropriateness of skills training in each culturally different setting.

Other skills training models have included a wide range of theories. Kagan developed a model for "interpersonal process recall" using video in counselor education. Triandis (1975) uses a "culture assimilator" to train persons about other cultures based on the attributions or assumptions they made about others and others make about them. Human relations skill training approaches based on the qualities of empathy, warmth, and genuineness have also been tried in multicultural settings. Goldstein (1981) developed structured learning skills that emphasize modeling, role-playing, and social reinforcement. This approach has had good success in multicultural settings, particularly among youth and students.

Although skills training has had a successful history, there are some limitations to this approach in multicultural settings that need to be acknowledged.

1. Skills training has grown in many different directions so that comparability across populations or cultures is difficult.
2. There is a danger that clients are fitted to the skills training technique rather than beginning with the needs of the particular client.
3. Applying skills learned in a laboratory to the outside world has been a continuing problem for skills training.
4. Defining the limits of skills in solving or managing a problem is also difficult to do, resulting in sometimes overestimating the importance of skills.
5. Skills training is a product of Westernized culture and reflects many of its culturally learned assumptions.
6. When skills training focuses on individuals as an isolated biosocial unit, it ignores the needs of collectivist cultures.
7. Where skills training requires the intervention of outsiders, it may not fit cultures who have a higher need for privacy within the family.
8. It is not always possible to identify the reinforcing event or reward in another culture accurately.
9. When expensive technical facilities are required for skill training, it may be too expensive for another culture.

Training is less expensive than learning by experience to work with other cultures. In many cases the arguments against training have been based on badly designed training approaches. Good skills training will not depend on stereotypes and half truths, it will have a balance of process and content goals.

Culture-centered counseling skills are directed toward applying standard and widely accepted basic counseling skills to each of the four synthetic cultures. By demonstrating four variations of each basic skill and by focusing on a person's cultural context, the goal is to help counselors match the right method with the right person at the right time in the right way. By rehearsing this adaptability in synthetic culture settings, the counselor is expected to develop a framework for dealing with the more complex contrasting cultures in the real world.

Chapter Four

Preparing to Learn Culture-Centered Skills

Major Objective:
To prepare counselors for planning and conducting a culture-centered counseling interview.

Secondary Objectives:
1. To describe a framework for planning a counseling interview.
2. To define the characteristics of good feedback in culture-centered interviews.
3. To practice feedback skills with the four synthetic cultures.

A good counselor seems to know just what to say at just the right time. It is easy to assume that good counselors are born with this ability. In fact, good counseling results from much practice and training, whether that work was done in a classroom or through years of self-taught practice. Counseling, like any other professional skill, is the result of hard work. Although most counselors will quickly recognize the importance of good skills, they may rely on their own reading, practice, and recovery from their own mistakes to learn those skills when working with culturally different clients. There is a better alternative to trial-and-error learning about culture-centered counseling, and that is through training.

Persons differ in their ability to do culture-centered counseling. If two counselors interview the same person at different times, the outcome of each interview may very well differ. Persons differ in their interviewing style, and in the way they interpret information to make decisions. If there is a great deal of inconsistency between counselors, then one or the other counselor may experience serious problems. Poor counseling is likely to result in failure to meet objectives, poor public relations, inadequate relationships, and charges of discrimination when working with culturally different clients.

PLANNING THE INTERVIEW

Good culture-centered counseling results from a high level of skills in managing the content and the process of the interview, which needs to cover the appropriate topics and ask the right questions to be successful. In addition, the good counselor must use effective communication skills to open up the culturally different client and draw out useful information. We have already discussed the importance of cultural awareness and knowledge to provide the basis for culture-centered skills in counseling

Good culture-centered counseling requires planning. The counselor must first know the objectives to be achieved. Second, the counselor needs to consider the appropriate approach and interview style. For example, should it be relaxed and conversational, or should it be more formal? Should the interview be highly structured with a long list of questions, or should there be no structure at all? Third, a format needs to be designed to prevent counselors from wasting time by repeating themselves or drifting off the topic. A list of topics or sample questions to be covered provides a helpful guide. This typical five-stage sequence for a culture-centered counseling interview provides an example:

1. *Initiation.* State the purpose of the interview and get the client to talk by using open-ended questions. However, in some cultures you may need to show your experience first.
2. *Listen.* Practice active listening so that you can bring these topics up later.
3. *Focus.* Direct attention to topics raised by the client for further clarification.
4. *Probe.* Pursue relevant topics raised or that seem to require extra attention to fill in gaps.
5. *Use.* Apply what you have learned from the interview to meet its objectives.

Interviewing or counseling is the most frequently used method for supervising and/or managing people in most, if not all, cultures. Interviewing may be done formally, with a specific objective, or informally, while getting to know the situation. Interviewing may be directed toward employees, peers, superiors, customers, or the general public as clients. Interviewing is different from ordinary conversation in that it involves purposeful communication with another person. The purpose may be exchanging information, getting ideas accepted, helping employees, solving problems, or making decisions such as selecting, orienting, training, developing, appraising, promoting, or terminating. While many people have a natural ability to interview, it is a skill that can be improved even among the best interviewers.

Interviewing and counseling deal with the human side of communication, where the complexity of problems, personalities, and situations eliminates easy answers. As cultural styles change from authority-centered, directive approaches to person-centered, participative ones, interviewing becomes a more important skill.

Good interviewing depends on a person's ability to go beyond standardized or programmed answers and make a special judgment with special communications skills in special situations. This book is directed toward presenting the principles and techniques of good counseling and interviewing in a practical format.

FEEDBACK SKILLS

In the process of practicing the culture-centered counseling skills described in this book, participants will need to give feedback to one another about observations, evaluations, and recommendations. It is appropriate to begin building skills by looking at giving feedback appropriately. If feedback is not given appropriately, interaction may have negative consequences. The content of the feedback may be accurate, but the way that content is given may not be appropriate. In order to be effective, both the content and process of feedback need to be appropriate.

Frequently the message sent is different from the message received. Feedback is the process of making sure that they are the same. Frequently feedback will respond to what persons said and did as well as what they did not say or do. Frequently the feedback will go beyond merely describing the message sent and include interpretations of that message as well as speculation about its consequences.

There are several standard guidelines for providing appropriate feedback:

1. Focus on a person's behavior, rather than on the person himself. If I tell someone, "You are a bad person," or even "You did that talk poorly," that feedback will not be useful nor will it likely lead to useful outcomes. There is more heat than light in a personal attack. If, instead, I tell that person, "You did not achieve the goals you went after yet," the feedback is more likely to be understood as it was intended and is more likely to lead toward the desired change.

2. Focus on observations rather than on inferences. We already discussed this in Chapter One. It is not always easy to separate fact from inference. One person might say, "I have not eaten," and you might infer the person is hungry—when in fact the person is not hungry. Many times we think we are giving feedback on facts when we are basing it on our own inferences. The "self-reference criterion" is the presumption that each person's own experi-

ences are appropriate reference points for understanding other people's experiences. Do *not* do onto others as you would have them do unto you, because they may want something *different!* Sympathy is how you would feel if it was happening to you. Empathy goes beyond sympathy to focus on what that other person is actually feeling.

3. Focus on description rather than judgment. Premature judgments of goodness or badness are some of the most frequent errors in giving feedback. First, you need to make sure that you can describe the message sent to the satisfaction of the sender. Value judgments require an accurate description of a situation. Usually our value judgments are made with very little data, especially with regard to culturally different persons. As a consequence we experience the goodness or badness that we expect, irrespective of the reality in each multicultural experience. For example, "When you interviewed that client, why did you interrupt just as he/she was able to get to the central issue?" A judgmental statement might be, "You really missed it there!"

4. Focus on the here and now, rather than on the there and then. If you focus on the present situation and what the person is saying or doing at the time, you can be more sure that you know what happens. Things that happened in the past become changed by interpretation and selective memory. Research on skill development suggests also that more immediate feedback is also more likely to result in change. The more abstract and distant in terms of time and space, the less likely that feedback will be understood as intended.

5. Focus on sharing information rather than giving advice. When giving feedback on a topic about which you have strong feelings, it is easy to argue your point and try to persuade the other person to agree with you. It is important to separate your advice-giving function from your need to provide important information to others. Where counseling and interviewing have been guilty of manipulation, it has usually been caused by inappropriate or self-referenced preaching or advice. It has frequently been the practice of counselors to "scratch where it doesn't itch"—to the frustration of the recipient.

6. Focus on what is said rather than on why it is said. It is difficult to determine the reason behind the message sent. It is sometimes even difficult to know our own reasons for saying and doing what we do. Guessing a person's motive is very speculative and likely to result in argument. By focusing first on the message itself, both of you can better understand the expectation accurately. The Cultural Grid discussed in Chapter Two provides a framework to move from clearly identified behaviors to the culturally learned expectations and values behind that behavior.

7. Focus on giving only as much information as a person can use. If you provide too much information in your feedback, it will not all be able to be absorbed. By keeping your feedback specific and to the point, it is much more likely to be understood and result in appropriate change. Because culture is so complex and dynamic, it is especially important in culture-centered counseling to focus your attention clearly and unambiguously.

8. Focus on information useful to the other person and not just useful to yourself. Sometimes people project their own anger at others under the pretense of giving helpful advice or feedback. The purpose of this feedback is more to meet the needs of the person giving it than the person receiving it. Counter-transference would be an example of a counselor reacting positively or negatively to a client. The counselor's expectations or attitudes are always shaped by the counselor's previous experiences.

EXERCISE 4.1: PRACTICE IN USING FEEDBACK SKILLS

In order to practice your use of feedback skills, it will be important for you to use them in a role-playing situation. The following situation will provide that opportunity:

1. Select two partners.
2. One of you will speak about his or her culture for one minute.
3. One of you will listen to the speaker carefully for one minute. When the speaker has completed his or her description, the listener will give feedback to the speaker for one minute on what the speaker said (facts and information), felt, and meant (why did the speaker say or do what he or she said or did?
4. The third person will be an observer and listen to both the speaker and the listener giving feedback. When both have completed their task, the observer will lead a discussion on how well the feedback process met the seven rules provided earlier in this chapter.
5. The group will now change roles so that the speaker becomes the listener, the listener becomes the observer, and the observer becomes the speaker.
6. When the second round has been completed, the group will change roles again so that each member will have the opportunity to experience all three.

In the following chapters you will have many opportunities to give feedback to your colleagues. It will be important for you to give accurate, timely, and useful feedback so that you may learn from one another.

GIVING FEEDBACK TO SYNTHETIC CULTURES

A positive and a negative simulated example of feedback skills will be presented and discussed for each of the four synthetic cultures: Alpha, Beta, Gamma, and Delta.

Giving Feedback to Alphas

Alpha culture emphasizes the unequal distribution of power in institutions and organizations in a hierarchy of privilege. Few people have much power and the vast majority has less. Alphas will be quiet, soft-spoken, and polite as you give feedback, but if they feel that you are being unfriendly, they will stop listening. Alphas will show their trust in you by asking for help and direction and will show their respect by remaining formal and lowering their eyes. When Alphas make direct eye contact or do not display positive and animated nonverbals, you have become boring and lost their respect. Alphas will not hesitate to talk but will be restrained and formal in their conversation, seeking to please you as best they can and accepting blame for any failure to please you. While they will internalize stress, they will give indirect signs of their stress and distress in their feedback to you.

It may be useful to consider several simulated counseling interviews where feedback is given to an Alpha client.

Alpha Interviews

Counselor: You seem to be unhappy. Can you tell me what's troubling you? (looking directly at the client)

Alpha: I'm fine. (looking downward)

Counselor: I think you're angry at me because of what I said to you several weeks ago.

Alpha: (silence)

Counselor: You need to become more open with your feelings and tell me exactly what you're thinking or we can never make progress.

Alpha: I'm sorry that I can't do that. (looking at the counselor directly)

Counselor: I'll be able to help you change if you'll let me.

Alpha: I'm sorry that you're so unhappy with me. (looking out the window)

Counselor: You don't seem to be paying attention to me. Are you angry at me right now?

Alpha: (sits silently, continuing to look out the window)

It is clear that the counselor violated the rules for giving good feedback by focusing on the past, by criticizing the person, rather than focusing on behavior, by focusing on inferences rather than observations, by making judgments, and in other ways. The counselor was also insensitive to the Alpha culture's indirect ways of giving feedback, however politely, which indicated a negative reaction of unfriendliness, distrust, disgust, and boredom. While the Alpha client was obligated to remain respectful and accept blame for any problems that occurred, the lack of trust and respect made any positive outcome from the feedback very unlikely.

It may be useful to examine a second example of giving feedback to an Alpha client which demonstrates a more successful outcome.

Counselor: You seem quiet today. Would it be appropriate for me to ask if something is bothering you?

Alpha: It's very kind of you to ask. (looking downward)

Counselor: (after a period of silence) When another Alpha client of mine had a problem, I was able to help solve it.

Alpha: That was good. I know about that person. (shaking his head up and down in agreement)

Counselor: Your caring about others is a good thing, like an older brother for a younger brother. (eyes lowered and speaking quietly)

Alpha: Perhaps you'll have the time to listen to my thinking about my younger brothers.

Counselor: You do me great honor by asking me.

Alpha: It's difficult for me to speak with outsiders about this thing.

Counselor: Sometimes being an outsider can be an advantage if the outsider cares for you.

Alpha: Yes, that's true, and I do believe you care.

Here the rules for providing feedback were followed, focusing on the person's behavior and observances with a minimum of inference, not being judgmental, focusing on the immediate present, not presuming to give advice or to push the client faster than desired, and focusing on the client's needs. The interview was also culture centered by following the client's lead in being soft-spoken and polite, allowing the client to ask for help with safety, and reducing the threat by speaking indirectly rather than directly to or about the client. The use of silence and supportive nonverbals was also helpful. Bringing in the hierarchy of family relationships also helped the client accept the outsider in a respectful and appropriate role.

Giving Feedback to Betas

Betas emphasize a high level of uncertainty avoidance and a lack of tolerance for ambiguity. They put a lot of emphasis on structure in their lives, defining duty to truth and the law as certain and absolute. They want clearly defined perspectives which are clean and not messy. They like a safe, predictable, tightly organized plan. When they are friendly, they will respond in detail, being formal and unambiguously specific. If they become unfriendly, they will become more generalized and ambiguous in their responses and seek to end the interview. If they trust you, they will debate and argue from either side of a polarized right/wrong, good/bad position, seeking to separate through argument. If they distrust you, they will be openly critical and challenge your credentials directly. They show interest by being very task oriented, verbal, and by asking many questions with direct eye contact. If they become bored, they will be passive and look away. They are good speakers, well organized, and verbal, although they sometimes are loud. They are animated in gestures but avoid physical contact. They have rigid beliefs which don't change easily. They will quickly—sometimes prematurely—

evaluate a situation to separate right from wrong. They don't have ulcers, but they give ulcers to others by externalizing stress.

Beta Interviews

Counselor: So, how do you want to begin?

Beta: You're the counselor. You tell me.

Counselor: I thought that maybe you would have an idea of what you wanted to talk about. (looking away from the client)

Beta: I want to know what to do so that I don't fail in my duty and responsibilities. I want you to tell me.

Counselor: That's an interesting insight. Maybe you want me to help you explore different solutions to your problem?

Beta: You keep trying to change the subject as though you don't want to tell me the truth! (waving arms to demonstrate frustration) I don't think you know what I should do. I don't think you're doing a very good job here! How long have you been counseling?

Counselor: You seem angry at me. We'll have to work together if we're going to solve your problems. I don't really know what you should do, but maybe we could explore possibilities.

Beta: If you don't know what I should be doing, then what in the world am I doing here? (gets up and walks toward the door)

Counselor: Please don't get so emotional. Try to go with the flow (reaches over to pat the client on his back)

Beta: I'm outta here! (leaves)

The counselor responded in a very ambiguous way when the client felt the counselor was neglecting responsibility. The counselor was trying to consult with the client as a coparticipant, and the client interpreted reflection as indecision or weakness. The client begins to form an opinion of the counselor as incompetent and challenges him. The counselor tries to redirect the client's anger toward the problem, and the client just becomes more frustrated. The counselor is judged as indecisive and weak. The admission of not knowing answers becomes the final straw for the client, who ends the interview. The counselor also violated many of the guidelines for good feedback by focusing on the client, rather than the client's behavior, making inferences, making judgments about the client in value-laden terms, and in getting defensive perhaps was focusing on the counselor's, rather than the client's, needs.

Let's look at a second example of giving feedback to a Beta client which has a more successful outcome.

Counselor: Please sit down over there, and I'll sit down here.

Beta: I need to know what's wrong with me and why I feel as I do.

Counselor: Tell me the three most important feelings that seem to be troubling you.

Beta: Let's see . . . I feel like I'm not being as responsible to my duties as I should be . . . I feel insecure and sort of anxious . . . and I need more structure to do the right thing. (looking directly at the counselor)

Counselor: First we'll look at your feeling not responsible to your duties. Which specific duties are a problem?

Beta: My wife and children don't obey me.

Counselor: So one of your problems relates to obedience in your family. Before we concentrate on the problem, let's look at the second problem you mentioned. You said you were feeling insecure and anxious. Why?

Beta: I always feel a little anxious. Right now I need to know what to do with my wife and children, so that my home can be a sure and certain refuge for our whole family and we can go back to a regular routine again.

Counselor: So you want me to tell you how to fix your family and restore the routine it once had where everybody knew their role and did what was expected of them? Is that accurate?

Beta: Yes, that's it exactly. (smiling and nodding his head vigorously)

Counselor: And now the third problem you mentioned was knowing exactly what to do next. You want a map or plan for what you should do to guarantee success. Is that right?

Beta: Exactly! That's exactly what I want! Do you think you can help me? (looking directly at the counselor)

Counselor: Okay, let's begin by analyzing each part of the situation. By telling me the details we can identify first what went wrong, second, why it went wrong, and third, what you need to do to fix it.

In this case the counselor provided a great deal more structure in the interview and allowed the Beta client to organize the problem more clearly using that structured framework. The client's concern about ambiguity and uncertainty was recognized, and the counselor responded in a rational series of steps to construct a clear picture of the problem. As a result the client was willing to be more detailed in responding and task oriented in procedure. The counselor also demonstrated good feedback technique by focusing on the person's behavior, detailing observations without making inferences, refraining from judging the client, focusing on what was being said, rather than why, and focusing on the client's, rather than the counselor's needs.

Giving Feedback to Gammas

Gamma culture emphasizes individualism and believes that people are supposed to take care of themselves while remaining emotionally independent of groups, organizations, or other collectivities. There is a lot of self-emphasis, even in building friendships. They can do whatever they want.

They build contracts to protect their rights from others and to protect their dignity. They have a high level of self-respect, but they enjoy a good time and an occasional adventure, even if they might feel guilty later. When they are friendly, they are very verbal and open, but they can be very critical and vengeful toward enemies. They like to debate issues and will struggle for control in a group they trust but will withdraw and become defensive if they distrust a group. They can be loud with lots of questions and lots of physical contact when they are interested, but they are likely to look away and walk off if they get bored. Sometimes they are perceived as flirting with the opposite sex as though they were trophy hunting. They are always on guard against potential enemies. They judge others by how much they need them. They like to live "on the edge" to prove how good they are.

Gamma Interviews

Let's look at an interview with a Gamma client where the counselor does not do a good job giving feedback.

Counselor: How are we feeling today? (smiling and leaning back in the chair)

Gamma: I'm probably not feeling as good as you seem to be feeling. (smiling sarcastically)

Counselor: (leaning forward over the desk and looking directly at the client) Are you embarrassed coming to see a counselor? You seem angry.

Gamma: I'm not angry . . . yet. And even if I am, that's my business.

Counselor: We aren't going to make much progress unless we work together. I've worked with lots of kids like you, and only those who worked together with me have been successful.

Gamma: (looking away) Why should I trust you? What's in it for me?

Counselor: You have an obligation to your family, to society, and a duty to make some sacrifices to help them like they help you.

Gamma: Nobody ever helped me, and even if they tried, I wouldn't let them. I don't want to owe anybody. I'm my own person.

Counselor: You don't want help, do you? You just sit right there until you're ready to talk with me and let me help you.

The counselor starts by prematurely presuming a unity between counselor and client. The client responds defensively, and the counselor gets defensive back. The counselor presumes a shared understanding of affiliative values which the client denies and which makes the counselor still more defensive. The counselor and client move steadily in opposite directions, with the counselor advocating obligations and the client advocating independence. The counselor also violates the guidelines for giving feedback by focusing on the person, rather than the person's behavior, to the point of almost attacking the client, making negative inferences without adequate data, giving unsolicited advice, and becoming defensive.

Let's look at a second interview between a counselor and a Gamma client with a somewhat more successful outcome.

Counselor: I'm glad to see you came. I've been reading about you and looking forward to meeting you.

Gamma: It's a little hard coming here. I'm afraid the other guys will find out and think I'm a sissy. Do you think I'm a sissy?

Counselor: No, I think you have real courage coming here to deal with your problem directly and take control. Let's make a bargain. I'll do as much as I can if you'll do as much as you can. Is it a deal?

Gamma: Sure. It's a deal. (they shake hands on it) Where do I start? What do you want me to do? What comes first?

Counselor: Good questions! You maybe already have some ideas about what works, so why don't you tell me what you think about the situation you're facing, and then I'll jump in when I have a question or something to add.

Gamma: Great! Maybe if you take one side and I take the other, we can find out what works.

The counselor shows respect and interest in the student as a person both by the way the client is addressed and by taking the trouble to do some homework before the interview. The client feels valued as an individual and willing to disclose some fears to the counselor that might have been unsafe otherwise. The client is not threatened and forms an alliance with the counselor against the problem. The client sees the counselor as potentially useful and sees counseling as an exciting challenge. The counselor follows many of the guidelines for giving feedback by basing any observations on the client's specific behavior and checking out any inferences. The counselor avoids making value judgments and focuses just on what was said, rather than why it was said.

Giving Feedback to Deltas

Deltas emphasize masculinity in their assertiveness and emphasis on money and material things, rather than value nurturance, quality of life, or the needs of other people. Deltas treat life as a competition. They fight aggressively to assert themselves and be winners. They believe themselves deserving and destined to excel—by force, if necessary. They like to show off by being the biggest, best, fastest there is. They are expected to flirt and like to be noticed when they come into the room. They like to dominate discussions and compete, especially if they win. They like sports and use sports metaphors to explain daily problems. They tend to argue and criticize others, even when they don't intend to antagonize them. They look up to heroes and scramble to increase their status whenever they can. They can never achieve enough and are always enthusiastic to succeed in whatever they do.

Delta Interviews

Let's look at an example of a counselor using feedback skills less successfully with a Delta client.

Counselor: I'm glad you came to me for help. Please sit down over there. (indicating a chair across the desk)

Delta: (taking a different chair beside the counselor) Well, I'm not glad, let me tell you! I don't want to be here one little bit.

Counselor: You certainly are frazzled. I've never seen you so upset. (leaning far back in the chair and looking at a file)

Delta: Hey, Mac, look at me! I just passed you the ball, and you fumbled it. You gotta pay attention if you're gonna win the game.

Counselor: You think we're playing a game here? You think I'm playing against you or something?

Delta: Everybody plays, nobody pays. Just catch the ball when I pass it, and feed off to me so I can shoot.

Counselor: I haven't a clue what you're talking about, but you sure seem like you're having a good time here at my expense. What's the big idea?

Delta: (looking out the window and not saying anything)

The counselor tried to impose an agenda on the client, and the client didn't like it. The counselor and client ended up competing for power in the interview, and the counselor lost. The counselor was not comfortable with the sports metaphors the client preferred to use and projected a picture of the client as a loser, and the client resented the implied put-down. The client quickly lost interest in the interview and gave up on the counselor as a source of help. The counselor got angry at the client, and this further isolated the counselor. The counselor also disregarded feedback guidelines by focusing on the person, rather than the person's behavior, and making ungrounded inferences and value judgments about the client. The counselor was uncomfortable and defensive, focusing more on the counselor's own needs than the client's.

Let's look at an interview where the counselor is more successful using feedback skills with a Delta client.

Counselor: How's it going? Come on in and sit over here by me, so we can talk together! (shaking hands and leading the client to two chairs close together) You want some coffee or anything?

Delta: No, thanks, but thanks for askin'. It's a bummer. I'm not feeling so good right now.

Counselor: Yeah, you look sad and hurtin'. I'm used to seeing you up there fightin' back and winnin' the games.

Delta: (smiling and shaking his head) Not today! No way! I've got problems. Maybe even you can't help me. (looking directly at the counselor)

Counselor: Give it a shot and let's see. We're on the same team here. What's the problem?

Delta: I'm gettin' bad grades here and havin' a hard time at school with the teachers.

Counselor: You're used to winning and now you're afraid of losing? Is that it?

Delta: Yeah . . . I wish it was just a ball game. I know how to win there, but this academic stuff . . . that's something else.

Counselor: Maybe some of the same things you use to win ball games can help you with the academic stuff. Let's get a handle on things here and talk about what needs to get done so you can get to feeling better. Okay?

The counselor here seems much more comfortable with the client in the client's own frame of references, using sports and competitive metaphors and helping reinforce the client's self-esteem. The counselor does not avoid physical contact and lets the client direct the conversation toward his own stated goals and objectives. The client's strengths are emphasized, and the challenge of being successful in academics is presented in terms he is likely to understand. The counselor also follows some of the guidelines for giving feedback by grounding every inference and observation in specific client behaviors, avoiding value judgments, and focusing on the present, here and now. The counselor works with the client by sharing information, rather than giving advice, and is focused on the client's needs, rather than the counselor's outside agenda.

CONCLUSION

The four different and contrasting synthetic cultures provide a wide range of alternatives for giving feedback successfully. It is important for counselors to be culture centered in their counseling skills. The cultural context is where the power is, where the client has learned the rules for making sense out of the world. It is impossible to reach the person in isolation from that culture, just as it is impossible to escape one's own cultural envelope. It is possible, however, to reach beyond culturally learned behaviors to the expectations and values behind them. It is possible to modify and translate counseling to each different culture, just as it is possible to translate language. As in language translation, there is never a perfect match, but a good translation can be understood as a valuable vehicle of communication.

As we discuss each of the following culture-centered counseling skills, we will demonstrate four contrasting applications of each according to the four synthetic cultures. There are, of course, many, many additional cultural variations beyond the few examples we will demonstrate, but these examples can provide the starting point for developing a culture-centered framework for translating counseling skills to fit a complex and dynamic multicultural setting.

KEY IDEAS

I. Planning the interview: Being able to know just what to say at just the right time.

    A. Means of learning about interviewing:
Natural-born facility.
Self-taught through trial and error.
Training in interviewing skills.

    B. Poor interviewing may result in:
Failure to meet the interview objectives.
Poor public/client relations.
Charges of discrimination and unfairness.

    C. Good interviewing may result from:
A high level of interviewing skill.
Managing the content of an interview.
Managing the process of an interview.
Good communication skills.

    D. Planning a good interview:
Develop clear objectives.
Know how objectives will be achieved.
Consider appropriate approach and style.
Avoid wasting time by drifting off the subject.

    E. Stages of interview planning:
Initiating the purpose of the interview.
Actively listening to interviewees.
Focusing on key topics for clarification.
Probing areas requiring special attention.
Using what you learned to meet objectives.

II. Feedback skills: Feedback is accurately matching message sent with message received.

    A. Judging the accuracy of feedback:
According to the content of feedback.
According to the process feedback uses.
According to what is said or done.
According to what was not said or done.

    B. Guidelines for providing appropriate feedback:
Focus feedback on the person's behavior.
Focus on observations, rather than inferences.
Focus on descriptions, rather than judgments.
Focus on the here and now, the immediate present.
Focus on sharing information, rather than advice.

Focus on what was said, rather than why.
Don't give too much information.
Focus on the other person's needs, rather than your own.

III. Giving feedback to synthetic cultures.

A. Giving feedback to Alpha:
Respect the hierarchy of power.
Be polite, quiet, and soft-spoken.
Encourage requests for help.
Be formal, and avoid direct eye contact.
Attend to indirect indications of stress.

B. Giving feedback to Beta:
Provide structure in your suggestions.
Respect rules of law and truth.
Offer clearly defined, specific perspectives.
Suggest safe, predictable, and well-organized ideas.
Encourage open debate without being defensive.
Be task oriented.

C. Giving feedback to Gamma:
Respect individual differences.
Respect each person's dignity and honor.
Encourage the debate of issues.
Look for self-interest of individuals.
Don't take flirting too seriously.
Make yourself indispensable to their best interests.

D. Giving feedback to Delta:
Expect assertiveness.
Recognize the value of money and material things.
Accept a competitive agenda.
Recognize the value of bigness, force, and speed.
Use metaphors of games, sports, and contests.
Emphasize winning outcomes.
Avoid outcomes that result in losing.
Allow arguments and criticism without defensiveness.
Recognize heroes and high status needs.

EXERCISE 4.2: FEEDBACK SKILLS

1. Divide the participants into three-person groups.
2. One person will be the speaker and talk about a significant event in his or her life.
3. One person will be the listener, who will repeat back to the speaker everything the speaker said, felt, and meant *in one minute.*
4. The third person will be the observer, who will complete the following checklist to evaluate the use of feedback skills used by the listener.

Instructions to the observer: Listen carefully as the listener repeats what the speaker said, felt, and meant. Write direct-quote comments, giving examples of how the listener used feedback skills.

1. Focus on *behavior*, rather than on the person.
Example:

2. Focus on *observations*, rather than on inferences.
Example:

3. Focus on *description*, rather than on judgment.
Example:

4. Focus on the *here and now*, rather than on the past or future.
Example:

5. Focus on *sharing information*, rather than on giving advice.
Example:

6. Focus on *what* was said, rather than why.
Example:

7. Focus on *enough* but not too much feedback.
Example:

8. Focus on the *other person's needs*, rather than on your own.
Example:

Chapter Five

Basic Attending Skills

Major Objective:
To identify the fundamental attending skills necessary for a successful culture-centered counseling interview.

Secondary Objectives:
1. To understand the purpose of verbal and nonverbal attending skills in a counseling interview.
2. To identify problems that might interfere with effective attending in a counseling interview.
3. To practice attending skills with the four synthetic cultures.

Attending is one of the most basic counseling skills. Simply put, *it is important to pay attention to what is happening and being said in the session.* Attending skills will help the interviewer encourage quiet persons to talk more and others to talk less. By attending the interviewer will demonstrate interest in what is being said, awareness of patterns in the interview, the ability to change patterns, and the meaning of an interview. Basic attending skills are the foundation on which all other interviewing skills are based, the facility to identify and interpret verbal and nonverbal messages through careful observation.

Derald Sue and David Sue (1990) describe differences in communication styles between Native Americans, Asian-Americans, Hispanics, European-Americans, and African-Americans to demonstrate the likelihood of miscommunication across these ethnic and racial boundaries when inadequate attending skills are used. They describe Native Americans as speaking more slowly and softly, using indirect gaze when listening or speaking, interjecting less and encouraging communication less, more likely to use silence or delayed auditory response, and using a manner of expression that is more low-keyed and indirect. Asian-Americans and Hispanics are characterized as speaking softly, avoiding eye contact when listening or speaking to high-status persons, depending on similar rules, using moderate delay in verbal response, and being low-keyed and indirect. African-Americans are characterized as speaking with affect, using prolonged direct eye contact when speaking but less when listening, interrupting or turn-taking when they can, being quicker in verbal responses, and being affective and emotional in their interpersonal responses. European-Americans are characterized as speaking loudly and rapidly in a controlling manner, using greater eye contact when listening, using head nods and nonverbal markers a lot, being quick in responding, and being objective and task-oriented. The contrasting and conflicting patterns of communication are obvious. It is easy to see how the same behavior by different ethnic groups might lead them each to misinterpret that behavior.

THE PURPOSE OF ATTENDING

The major function of attending skills is to encourage the client to talk. Given that some cultures are less verbal, it might be appropriate to modify that function slightly to helping the client disclose, verbally and/or nonverbally, directly and/or indirectly, the patterns that give a situation meaning. Both verbal and nonverbal communication are equally important to the attending counselor. The message sent and the message received are quite often very different from one another.

EXERCISE 5.1: MESSAGE SENT AND MESSAGE RECEIVED

The objective of this exercise is to compare the differences between messages sent and messages received across cultures.

1. Select a partner who is different from yourself in nationality, ethnicity, gender, age, socioeconomic status, or some other significant social-system variable.

2. Identify a situation that happened to you in the past where you had strong feelings about that particular aspect of yourself that is different from your partner.

3. Describe the situation to your partner in three to five minutes without interruption or until you have said everything you have to say about the situation.

4. Both you and your partner will then score the extent to which *you* were experiencing the following feelings *both* (1) at the time you experienced the event, *and* (2) at the time you told it to your partner. Score the extent of your feelings on each scale with a 10 indicating a very high level of feeling and a 1 indicating a very low level. Circle the score indicating what you felt at the

time of the event and check the score indicating your feeling at the time you told it to your partner. These scores may or may not be the same.

Love	1	2	3	4	5	6	7	8	9	10
Happiness	1	2	3	4	5	6	7	8	9	10
Fear	1	2	3	4	5	6	7	8	9	10
Anger	1	2	3	4	5	6	7	8	9	10
Contempt	1	2	3	4	5	6	7	8	9	10
Mirth	1	2	3	4	5	6	7	8	9	10
Surprise	1	2	3	4	5	6	7	8	9	10
Suffering	1	2	3	4	5	6	7	8	9	10
Determination	1	2	3	4	5	6	7	8	9	10
Disgust	1	2	3	4	5	6	7	8	9	10

Compare your scores to your partner's. Did they match? Where did your partner think you had more or less feeling, and why?

Now ask your partner to repeat this process by telling you a story. Discuss the patterns of similarity and difference between the messages each of you sent and the messages each of you received.

Ivey (1988) identifies four foundation dimensions of attending that give structure to this skill area.

1. The first dimension is the use of the eyes. In some cultures direct eye contact is desired, in other cultures it is not. In all cultures the eyes are used to convey meaning and interest. The client's pattern of preference in using eye contact should be noted early and modeled by the counselor.

2. The second dimension is the use of body language. While this is more ambiguous and difficult to interpret, it is always very important and must be attended to. In most cultures what you do and what you do not do will be interpreted. If your verbal message is saying one thing and your body language is saying something else, the body language is more likely to be believed. Pay attention to the client's body language, and when you are not sure whether yours is communicating your meaning accurately, ask the client discretely. The feedback skills discussed in the previous chapter will help you find ways to check out your own explicit and implicit messages.

3. The third dimension is vocal qualities. Your tone of voice and speech rate will communicate your feelings about the other person—perhaps even more clearly than you would like. This will be especially important

when you or the client are not using a native language. One message can take on a full range of positive and negative meanings just by changing tone and speech rate.

4. The fourth dimension is verbal tracking. Staying with a client is essential, however complicated, confusing, or indirect the wandering conversation might become. If possible it is better not to change the subject but to stay with clients on their own terms until they are satisfied that they have told you what they want or need to. Culturally different clients who are suspicious might test you by deliberately being indirect until they are confident that you will be helpful. Remember, even though the material may not make sense to you, it may very well make sense to the client, and eventually you may discover hidden meanings that a less patient counselor would have missed.

Verbal attending skills relate to an accurate interpretation of how the words in an interview are used. A skilled interviewer will notice patterns and changes in patterns of verbal behavior, such as changes in pitch, volume, and speech rate. The good interviewer will notice when special emphasis is placed on a word or phrase as a form of verbal underlining. A skilled interviewer will notice hesitations and breaks in responses and know that these have meaning.

Verbal attending skills help the interviewer to track the interviewee. Notice the selective attention to some topics, key phrases, or words. Notice patterns of responses unique to that person. Notice who changes the subject and when. Look for uncomfortable moments in the interview, and examine exactly what was happening then.

Erickson and Schultz (1982) looked at uncomfortable moments in interviews where the counselor was from one culture and the client from another. They discovered that when counselors and clients shared a co-membership that might include nationality, ethnicity, gender, age, residence, or life-style, there were fewer uncomfortable moments, while clients and counselors who lacked this common ground were more frequently troubled by uncomfortable moments. The uncomfortable moments were brief interludes of awkwardness or uncertainty regarding what each could expect of the other. These are most common in cross-cultural counseling.

In order to understand the uncomfortable moments in cross-cultural counseling, it is important to look at behavior, expectations, and barriers across cultures.

In Chapter Three we reviewed the four synthetic cultures. The following table (5.1) will demonstrate the importance of accurately matching behaviors to expectations for each of these contrasting viewpoints. This table illustrates how similar behaviors can have very different meanings in different cultures. An Alpha will be polite even when being unfriendly. Betas will become more vague and general as they move from being friendly to unfriendly. Gammas

Table 5.1 Expectation and Behavior

Expectations	Behaviors			
	Alphas	**Betas**	**Gammas**	**Deltas**
Friendly	polite and listening	formal and specific	verbal and disclosing	physical, loud
Unfriendly	polite and not listening	general and ambiguous	critical, attacking	sarcastic, distant
Trust	asks for help	actively debates	debates and competes	challenges
Distrust	does not ask for help	attacks and challenges	noncommittal, passive	critical, insulting
Interest	positive, no eye contact	active with eye contact	loud and physical	playful
Boredom	passive, direct eye contact	passive, no eye contact	distant, quiet	detached, distant

will be verbal whether they are friendly or not. Deltas will be loud whether they are friendly or not. To show trust the Alphas will accept help, the Betas debate you, the Gammas and Deltas compete with you. Alphas will show their interest through direct eye contact; Gammas and Deltas will show their interest by being loud and physical. In some cases the behavior means opposite or contrary expectations in the different cultures.

A comparison of how these four synthetic cultures use the typical barriers to communication across cultures will also demonstrate the importance of attending carefully. Barna (1982) discusses these barriers as "stumbling blocks" to intercultural communication. She contends that our tendency to assume similarity instead of difference when communicating across cultures will most likely become a barrier to communication. In addition she cites five other barriers: language, nonverbals, stereotypes, evaluation, and stress. Pedersen (1985) has added organizational constraints, which might prevent communication even among culturally different people who are ready and willing to communicate. Let us compare these barriers with regard to the four synthetic cultures (see Table 5.2).

In attending to persons from another culture, it is essential to focus on the different ways that each barrier functions for each cultural group. These are not barriers for those within the same culture where everyone knows the rules. They become barriers only when persons from outside that culture attempt to communicate across cultural boundaries without knowing the rules. Attending to different behaviors is not, by itself, enough. It is important to attend to the patterns, barriers, expectations, and meanings behind a culturally different person's behavior.

Table 5.2 Barriers

Barrier	Synthetic Cultures			
	Alpha	**Beta**	**Gamma**	**Delta**
Language	Verbal and soft-spoken	Loud and verbal	Verbal, self-centered	Critical, argumentative
Nonverbals	Restrained and formal	Animated, nonphysical	Seductive, physical	Physical, direct
Stereotypes	Hierarchical, pleasing	Rigid beliefs	Defensive, paranoid	Macho, hero-oriented
Evaluation	Self-blaming	Premature evaluators	Utilitarian, selfish	Overachievers
Stress	Internalizes stress	Externalizes stress	Risk-takers	Generates stress
Organizational Constraints	Formal rules	Highly structured	Disorganized, chaotic	Competes to win

THE PROCESS OF VERBAL AND NONVERBAL ATTENDING

Ordinarily the interviewer's verbal responses will be warm and expressive, communicating interest and involvement in what is happening. They will follow from what the interviewee is saying, showing continuity. The interviewer will not normally change the topic or interrupt. The interviewer will not normally provide an immediate answer or solution to a question or problem—at least not without thoroughly understanding the situation. The interviewer will normally focus on and follow what the interviewee is saying with as much detailed attention as possible.

Sometimes silence also becomes an important means of communication. Silence can have as wide a range of qualities and messages as noise in the communication process. There can be a comfortable and relaxing silence, and there can be a tense or anxious silence. In many cultures clients will go inside themselves for help with a problem and think back to proverbs or basic truths taught to them when they were young. Only when these inner resources have failed them might they consider going to an outsider like a counselor for help.

Most American counselors tend to be uncomfortable with silence. In one university counseling center all the international students from a particular culture were being diagnosed as distracted because they would not respond to a question immediately. In that particular culture a thirty-second or brief period of silence was a mark of respect and a sign that what had been said was being considered carefully. It would be useful for counselors to practice being comfortable with silence so that, should the occasion arise, they will be able to match that mode of communication by a client.

Nonverbal attending skills include attention to body language, the many nonverbal ways we communicate by posture and gestures. In many Western cultures leaning forward slightly is interpreted as being both interested and attentive, while other cultures will place a contrasting interpretation on the same behavior. It is important to establish a comfortable distance in the interview, with some cultures preferring more distance and others less.

As clients shift and change their body language, the interviewer may reflect on the interview at that point to determine why the change occurred. By matching the interviewer's pattern of body language to mirror the interviewee's, the client is likely to feel more comfortable and understood. Body posture should always, however, be natural, attentive, and relaxed to communicate interest. Gestures should also be easy and natural according to the interviewer's own style.

Nonverbal attending skills also include eye contact. A person's pupils will dilate when interested and become smaller when threatened. Notice breaks in eye contact and how the client looks away when distressed. Notice whether direct eye contact is appropriate or not. Eye contact should be natural without staring. It should communicate that you are attending to the interview. The eye contact should be more or less constant depending on the culture.

It is especially important to notice discrepancies, incongruities, mixed messages, contradictions, and other inconsistencies in the interviewee's verbal and/or nonverbal behavior. Each verbal and/or nonverbal behavior contains a hidden message. For example, interpret the following nonverbal messages communicated by body language:

Crossed arms and/or legs

Rapid shift of eye contact

Stammering or speech hesitation

Furrowed eyebrows

Lips tighten (or loosen)

Flushing of the face and changes in color

Rate of breathing changes

Pupils dilate or contract

Talking casually with clenched fists.

Verbal behaviors can also take on a special meaning. Interpret the following in terms of their hidden messages:

Stays on a single topic to the exclusion of everything else

Changes the topic subtly or abruptly

Excessive talking about themselves

Repetition of key words or concepts

Emphasizes some words more than others

Makes two statements that don't agree

Says one thing but does another

Suddenly becomes quiet and stops talking

As a general rule attending skills should help you focus on the person being interviewed without becoming overly self-conscious. The interviewer needs to know his or her own most comfortable patterns of attending. At the same time, interviewers need to develop alternative attending patterns to fit the needs of different clients. By attending, the interviewer will perceive cues that tell when a behavior is appropriate or not. Finally, it is important not to be so distracted by the attending process that you lose track of what is happening in the interview.

Initially you will be focusing so carefully on learning specific attending skills that you will sometimes forget about the client entirely. In the initial stages of training it is not uncommon for a person's skills to actually drop while that person is imitating a model or trying to remember what should be done, losing the naturalness of personal style. Through practice, attending skills will eventually become much more natural and require less conscious thought. This is especially true as you learn to adapt your skills to contrasting cultural settings. However, by having examined each component of your culture-centered counseling skills and become familiar with the variety of ways they can be used, you will have increased your repertoire of possible skills to match the needs of culturally different clients.

A usually reliable measure of how well you are doing with a culturally different client can be found in monitoring your own comfort level. If you are uncomfortable and anxious, there is a pretty good chance you are communicating that to the client, and the client is also becoming anxious. If you are feeling at ease and comfortable, that will also be communicated and reflected in the client's own feelings about the situation.

The next step is to practice your attending skills using the four synthetic cultures as a framework. Practice both in group and one-on-one counseling settings.

EXERCISE 5.2: SYNTHETIC CULTURE GROUPS

If you videotaped the exercise where consultants visited synthetic cultures to help them deal with the problem of outsiders, those videotapes will provide a valuable resource to sharpen your attending skills.

Play back a ten-minute videotape from the earlier simulation showing a small group of persons from one synthetic culture working with a team of consultants from a contrasting culture. As you view the tape, attend to specific examples of significant behavior regarding the following:

Eye contact. Was direct eye contact appropriate or inappropriate? Who looked at whom? What meanings were you able to infer from attending to eye contact? What patterns of eye contact did you observe among the visitors and the host culture?

Body language. What were the differences in body language between the visitors and the host culture? What patterns did you observe?

Vocal qualities. What were the differences in vocal qualities between the visitors and the host culture, and what was the effect of those differences? What patterns of vocal quality did you observe, and what was their meaning?

Verbal tracking. How well did the visitors and the host culture follow one another in their communication? How often was there a change in topic, and who initiated it?

Silence. Were there moments of silence in the interview? What was happening during that silence? Was it helpful to the interview?

Uncomfortable moments. Was there an uncomfortable moment when the persons seemed unsure of what was expected of them and what they might expect from others? What exactly happened? What was the effect?

EXERCISE 5.3: SYNTHETIC CULTURE INTERVIEWING

It is useful to practice attending skills in a dyad relationship as well as in group observation.

1. Select one of the four synthetic cultures that you can role-play with authenticity.

2. Select a partner who is comfortable role-playing one of the other synthetic cultures.

3. Carry on a five-minute conversation together about the importance—or unimportance—of cultural differences in the counseling process or some other topic of mutual interest and importance.

4. Debrief one another by examining the way each of you attended to eye movements, body language, vocal qualities, verbal tracking, silence, and uncomfortable moments.

5. Provide feedback to one another about the degree to which you were accurate in attending to each factor and on how accurate and authentic you were in role-playing your synthetic cultures. Review the rules for your synthetic cultures, and identify any special patterns to look for in attending to the behavior of persons from them.

THE CONCEPTUAL BASIS OF ATTENDING

In the research literature on patterns of similarity and differences across cultures, the term "emic" (from phonemic) refers to aspects of a language that are unique and "etic" (from phonetic) refers to those that are universal. These terms were used by the anthropologist Pike (1967) to distinguish between the culture-unique (emic) and culture-general (etic) characteristics in a multicultural situation. We will be using the words unique or culture-specific instead of emic, and universal or cultural-general instead of etic in this book. It is important to look at both similarities and differences to get a balanced perspective of the relationship between two cultures. The problem has been that the more powerful culture has tended to impose its unique features as though they were universal at the expense of the less powerful cultures, who are forced to follow.

Those cross-cultural researchers and counselors who did not want to participate in this form of imperialism were frequently so self-conscious about differences between themselves and their clients that they were unable to function effectively. Berry (1969) suggested that cross-cultural researchers and service providers begin with the recognition that their instruments, methods, and assumptions are almost certainly biased. Consequently, they should go into a situation doing the best they can with instruments, methods, and perspectives admittedly rooted in a home culture or brought in from outside. Berry called this approach an "imposed universal." As the researcher or service provider becomes aware of the specific biases in an instrument, method, or assumption, those aspects can be modified and changed appropriately to fit the host culture and create more harmony. Therefore, instead of being *accidentally* biased, the service provider comes in *deliberately* biased but with a willingness and an eagerness to eliminate that bias as it is discovered. The measure of skill then becomes the ability to adapt outside instruments, methods, and assumptions to a host culture appropriately. In this way cultural differences are not allowed to immobilize the outsider. Biases can be removed as quickly as they are identified.

In practicing attending skills it is important to look at both similarities and differences. It is important to go beyond looking only at behaviors and, referring to the Cultural Grid in Chapter Two, look at shared expectations to build a platform of common ground between contrasting cultures. By attending carefully to behaviors and expectations it becomes possible to understand what is going on and to build culture-centered counseling skills for making a positive difference.

KEY IDEAS

1.   The purpose of attending skills.
        To encourage quiet persons to talk more.
        To encourage more talkative persons to speak less.

To demonstrate the interviewer's interest in what is said.
To identify patterns that repeat themselves.
To understand deeper meanings in the interview.
To identify and interpret verbal messages.
To identify and interpret nonverbal messages.
The role of expectations and behaviors.
The role of cultural barriers.

2. Verbal attending skills and behaviors.
Notice patterns of verbal behavior such as changes in pitch, volume, and speech rate during the interview.
Notice special emphasis on a word or phrase as verbal underlining.
Notice hesitations or breaks in responses.
Notice selective attention to some topics.
Notice key words or phrases that are used often.
Notice patterns of unique response.
Notice who changes the subject and when.
Notice uncomfortable moments in the interview.
Responses should be warm and expressive.
Responses should communicate interest and involvement.
Responses should follow what was said.
Responses should not normally interrupt.

3. Nonverbal attending skills and behaviors.
Include attention to eye movements.
Attend to body language.
Establish a comfortable distance.
Match and mirror changes in the other person's body language.
Sit in a way that is natural if possible.
Be attentive and relaxed.
Gestures should be easy and natural.
Use culturally appropriate gestures as you become aware of them.

4. The conceptual basis of attending.
Focus on the person being interviewed, rather than yourself.
Know your own most comfortable patterns of attending.
Develop alternative/contrasting patterns for different clients.
Listen/watch for cues that tell you if a behavior is appropriate.
Don't be distracted by the attending process itself.

EXERCISE 5.4: PRACTICE IN USING BASIC ATTENDING SKILLS

By practicing these basic attending skills you will at first be so self-conscious that it will make the interview more difficult. After practicing the attending skills more, however, they will become a more natural and automatic part of your style, making the interview less difficult.

Follow this sequence in practicing the use of attending skills:

1. Select two partners.
2. One of you will become an interviewer, who will play that role in a normal manner.
3. One of you will become an interviewee, who will take on one of the synthetic culture roles.
4. The last of you will become an observer, who will take notes on examples of verbal and nonverbal attending or nonattending behaviors by the interviewer.
5. The three of you will participate in a ten-minute role-played interview on a topic and setting to be provided.
6. At the end of the interview the observer will lead a ten-minute discussion, giving feedback to the others on specific examples of attending and nonattending behaviors.
7. At the end of the debriefing the members will change roles and repeat the process until all three have had an opportunity to be interviewer, interviewee, and observer.

Instructions to the observer: Listen and watch for specific examples of where attending skills were or were not used appropriately during the interview.

1. Responses were warm and expressive.
   Example:

2. Responses communicated interest and involvement.
   Example:

3. Responses followed a pattern without interruption.
   Example:

4. Responses focused on what the interviewee was saying.
   Example:

5. Responses attended to the interviewee's body language.
   Example:

6. Responses mirrored and matched the interviewee's.
   Example:

7. Responses showed both persons were attentive and relaxed.
   Example:

8. Responses used eye contact.
   Example:

9. Responses focused on the interviewee, rather than on the interviewer.
   Example:

10. Responses were easy, natural, and comfortable.
    Example:

11. Responses picked up on verbal/nonverbal cues.
    Example:

12. Responses were not distracted by the attending process.
    Example:

13. What are your overall impressions about the counselor's use of attending skills?

_____

Chapter Six

Paraphrasing, Summarizing, and Encouraging Skills

Major Objective:
To identify skills that will demonstrate to a culturally different client that he or she is being heard accurately.

Secondary Objectives:
1. To paraphrase or synthesize the essential message of a culturally different client.
2. To summarize or highlight the general message of a culturally different client.
3. To encourage or facilitate the counseling process with a culturally different client.

By encouraging, paraphrasing, and summarizing what has been said in the interview, the interviewer demonstrates that he or she has heard what went on. The interviewee will feel more understood and be more willing to further develop ideas as the interview progresses. These skills will also help the interviewer clarify what has been said and verify accuracy by checking out the interviewer's own perception. They will also make it less necessary for interviewees to repeat themselves and go over the same material more than once, thereby making the interview more efficient.

PARAPHRASING

The purpose of paraphrasing is to give feedback on the essence of what was said, putting that message in the interviewer's own words, including key words or phrases of special importance. The essence of what was said is repeated back in shortened form, providing clarification where necessary to fill in the gaps. If you are accurate, the client will validate your paraphrase with a statement such as, "That's right!" Accurate paraphrasing allows the interviewee to move on to new material with confidence. It can facilitate the exploration and clarification of issues. Tone of voice and body language can become important parts of paraphrasing, as in the use of key words or phrases. The main emphasis of paraphrasing is on the interviewee's viewpoint and checking out the accuracy of your perception.

In order to paraphrase accurately it is important to recall the interviewee's message, identify the essence of that message, and finally translate it into your own words. Be particularly careful, however, to use the client's most important key words and phrases. As an example of paraphrasing, attempt to repeat the essence of these last paragraphs to a partner.

EXERCISE 6.1: DIALOGUE WITHIN OURSELVES

In order to practice the skill, begin by paraphrasing your own internal dialogue. This will give you practice in listening to and making cultural interpretations of the internal dialogues of others on a given cross-cultural issue that generates ambivalent thoughts and feelings.

1. Select a cultural topic that produces ambivalent thoughts and feelings within you.
2. Concentrate on your own ambivalent thoughts, and listen to the two sides of your internal dialogue (on the one hand . . . on the other hand).
3. Write down as a dialogue your internal voices, attempting to identify the patterns of argument being used by both sides.
4. Judge which side of the argument you believe to be more persuasive and convincing, and ask yourself why.
5. What were the problems you encountered in being accurate in paraphrasing your own internal dialogue, and how might those same problems be overcome in paraphrasing someone else's perspective?

SUMMARIZING

Summarizations are longer than paraphrases and contain more information. They are usually used only at the beginning or end of an interview. Sometimes the interviewer will use a summary as a form of transition when it is necessary to change the topic. Summarization can be very helpful when you have a new client who gives you considerable information all at once. It is easy for even the most skilled to confuse a new client's complex story. Thus, stop the client and say back what you have heard. Then ask, "Have I heard you correctly?" or "What have I missed?" This will enable the client to correct you as necessary.

Summarizations usually cover a longer period of time, such as a whole interview or even several interviews. The summary includes both the verbal and nonverbal messages being sent or received. As a test of your ability, attempt to summarize the events that have happened so far in this class to your partners, and check out your accuracy with one another.

EXERCISE 6.2: SUMMARIZING AS A FORM OF STORYTELLING

Many ethnic groups use storytelling as a major vehicle in disseminating their culture. Many of these cultures lost the art with the coming of mass-produced printed communication and the media. Storytelling, however, assists us in learning the skills of summarizing by beginning with our own personal stories. In this way we summarize who we are and get to know ourselves better. In storytelling we perceive ourselves perceiving and we come to know ourselves knowing. We account for the events, joys, sorrows, and ceremonies that have made us uniquely ourselves and transmit our culture.

Form groups of three to five persons who will work together in doing this exercise. As you perform it, summarize specifically those people or events that have shaped your cultural identity.

1. Using large sheets of paper and crayons or markers, draw your culture, using symbols, sketches, pictures, and designs that represent the events, joys, sorrows, decisions, and such that have contributed to your unique development. You may not use words, but you may draw any other figure.

2. Now, looking over your story, place a plus sign by one event that you consider a highly positive factor. Next place a minus sign by one event you believe was an extremely negative experience.

3. Stand up in front of your group and tell your story. First, hang the drawing where everyone in the group can see it. Describe each element, design, picture, and symbol on your paper in terms of the unique meaning it had in the development of your own cultural identity. Give special attention to the items labeled with a plus and minus sign.

4. In attempting to understand the dynamics of these experiences, summarize which variables were influential in creating a positive or negative impact. Attempt to explain why those variables were so important.

5. Discuss the importance of culturally learned stories in the formation of our own identities.

EXERCISE 6.3: CULTURALLY LEARNED PATTERNS OF ENCOURAGERS

Biases are important barriers to cross-cultural communication. We tend to encourage persons who share our cultural point of view and criticize those who take a different viewpoint. We are trapped by our culturally learned patterns of encouragers unless we can escape this rigid set of rules. We can escape by becoming more aware of our cultural biases so that we will not be unintentionally controlled by them. In learning about how encouragers work it is important to identify implicit cultural biases and work out a strategy not to be rigidly controlled by them.

Circle five adjectives in the list below describing kinds of people you like, and underline five adjectives describing people you do not like to be around. You may add adjectives of your own if they are not included. Whenever possible relate each adjective to a particular group or culture.

adventurous	independent	shy
affectionate	indifferent	soft on subordinates
ambitious	influenced easily	stern
angered easily	intolerant	submissive
appreciative	jealous	successful
argumentative	kind	sympathetic
competitive	loud	tactful
complaining	neat	talkative
considerate	needs much praise	teasing
discouraged easily	obedient	thorough
discourteous	optimistic	thoughtful
distant	orderly	touchy
dominating	praise giving	trusting
efficient	rebellious	uncommunicative
enthusiastic	responsible	understanding
false	sarcastic	varied interests
forgiving	self-centered	very dependent
fun-loving	self-respecting	warm
good listener	self-satisfied	well-mannered
helpful	shrewd, devious	willing worker

Adapted from A. Pedersen, 1985.

ENCOURAGERS

Encouragers may include head nods, open-handed gestures, the saying of "um hmmm," the repetition of key words, or some other means of reassuring the interviewee without interrupting the interview. Even silence can be an encourager. The object of encouragers is to interrupt the interview as little as possible and to encourage the interviewee to keep talking. Excessive use of encouragers can be annoying to the interviewee if they become too forced or not spontaneous. As a test of your ability to use encouragers, provide feedback to your partners giving specific examples of when they have been encouraging to you or someone else so far during the class.

This is the simplest of the listening skills—but it is also one of the most powerful. Research indicates that effective and experienced counselors use this skill significantly more often than ineffective and inexperienced helpers.

SKILL BUILDING

If attending skills are listening and paying attention to a client, then the skills of paraphrasing, summarizing, and encouraging demonstrate feedback of what you have observed to check out the accuracy of your interpretation. In giving feedback to the client it is important to include both verbal and nonverbal observations. This is particularly important if you are not acquainted with the client's culture(s). As you report back to the client what you have heard and observed, it is important to identify:

1. patterns of repeated behaviors and ideas that keep coming up in different situations,

2. a comprehensive picture of the other person that does not overinterpret or underinterpret any isolated aspects of what you observed, and

3. discrepancies, incongruities, mixed messages, conflicts, or controversies that became apparent as you listened and observed.

These factors will tell their own story to you, and you must be faithful in telling that story accurately back to the client for analysis and interpretation.

In building on the attending and feedback skills of Chapters Three and Four, it is important to review in your own mind the content of your paraphrase or summarization. Think back on a particular interview you had with a culturally different client and your own use of paraphrasing and summarization in that interview relative to the following factors:

1. *Tracking.* Were you able to stay on the track of the client's train of thought? Did your attention wander, and if so when? Why?

2. *Nonverbals.* Was your eye contact facilitative? Was your body language facilitative? Were the vocal qualities you used facilitative? Were there any unintended nonverbal cues?

3. *Barriers.* Did you have any difficulties with the cultural barriers mentioned earlier: stress, language, nonverbals, evaluation, stereotyping, or organizational constraints?

4. *Value assumptions.* What are some examples of value assumptions that you shared with the client? What are some examples of value assumptions that were different? How did those value assumptions affect your interview?

5. *Inferences.* What are some examples of inferences you made about the interviewee, and where did those inferences come from?

6. *Discrepancies.* Were you able to relay discrepancies accurately back to the interviewee? How did awareness of those discrepancies influence the interview?

EXERCISE 6.4: SPECIAL INSTRUCTIONS TO THE INTERVIEWEE

Role-play a brief ten-minute interview in which the interviewee follows one of the following special instructions. The counselor's task will be to identify the pattern of behavior and give feedback to the client using paraphrasing and summarizing. These instructions are intended to provide specific patterns that will test the interviewer's attending skills. The interviewee should select one of the following seven patterns and follow it in the interview. The interviewee should not reveal which pattern is being followed until after the interview is completed.

1. Change the topic in subtle but significantly different directions at least once each minute or two. You should have changed the topic at least five times during the interview.

2. Match your own nonverbal behaviors (eye contact, body language, and vocal qualities) to the interviewer's as closely as possible. As these behaviors change for the interviewer, change yours accordingly.

3. Do not match the nonverbal behaviors of the interviewer. If the interviewer changes to match your behavior, change your behavior accordingly.

4. Include specific mention of how each barrier (stress, language, nonverbal, evaluation, stereotypes, and organizational constraints) has in turn contributed to your problem. Include these references in subtle ways.

5. Respond positively to at least one value assumption made by the interviewer, indicating that you share it. Respond negatively to at least one value assumption, indicating that you do not share it.

6. When the interviewer includes concrete, specific, and factual statements in the interview, react positively (smile, lean forward, show agreement and enthusiasm).

7. When the interviewer includes abstract, general, and inferential statements in the interview, react negatively (frown, lean backward, show disagreement and disappointment).

The above exercise should demonstrate that paraphrasing, summarizing, and encouraging are not random but shaped by the counselor's own culture and in part by the client's culture. It is important to identify patterns in the counselor's use of paraphrasing, summarizing, and encouraging so that the counselor will not be trapped into perpetuating an implicit transference of cultural teachings. For example, counselors may encourage clients to talk more about sexual behaviors, parenting, relationships, cognitive dilemmas, or a countless list of other factors of which the counselors themselves might not be aware. For this reason it is essential that counselors be aware of their own cultural patterns as the first step in the culture-centered counseling of culturally different clients. It is important to check out your accuracy after every paraphrase and summary statement to make sure that the message sent was the same as the one received.

In the following presenting-problem statements by four clients, indicate when you would use encouragers by writing on the transcript. Indicate what sort of paraphrasing you would do by filling in the brief spaces indicated. At the end of the presenting problem, outline how you would summarize what the client has told you.

THE ALPHA CLIENT

I am very sorry to trouble you, but my family thought that I should make an appointment with you because of your reputation as a wise and experienced counselor. I hope you understand how hard it is for me to come and talk with you about personal problems. If I hesitate or am unclear, I apologize. I want very much to be a good client and to please you.
(Paraphrase)

My problem is that persons I work with often take advantage of me. I like to protect the people working under me, to be helpful to my coworkers and to obey my supervisors, but I think they interpret my pleasing them as a sign of weakness, rather than as a sign of respect. They often complain to me about one another and force me to become involved in their negotiations for changing things. If I show any reluctance, they criticize me and say that I am only pretending to be their friend.
(Paraphrase)

They are also angry because I am reluctant to ask them for help. They say that my always wanting to give help but never wanting to receive help is not right. But I can't ask them for help if I don't trust them. They say that I act sneaky, never looking at them straight in the eye, and they say that they can't trust that kind of behavior, and it makes me so frustrated! I feel like a tree uprooted by the flood and being washed downstream. I really don't know what I can do or where to start. Can you help me?

(Summarize)

Answer the following questions or discuss them with your partner:

1. Where did you mark in encouragers, and why?
2. Check your paraphrasing against the rules for Alpha's culture to see if you were sensitive to it.
3. Check your summary against the rules for Alpha's culture to see if you were sensitive to it.

THE BETA CLIENT

I called the Psychological Association, and they gave me your name as a competent service provider in this district. I notice that—according to the certificates on your wall—you have a degree in counseling and that you are experienced. That is good. I need your advice. When I walk out of here I want a list of things to do that will improve my ability to get my staff to work with me better.
(Paraphrase)

My staff does not follow the rules as well as I would like, so there is no clearly defined principle that we can all count on to be followed. They tend to criticize me for being right, but since I know I am right, why shouldn't I stay with what I believe to be true?
(Paraphrase)

It is very frustrating to see my staff not taking things as seriously as they should. It is very frustrating when sometimes I find orders are not carried out as I had expected. It is very frustrating to have them complain about my being the leader, even though I am their boss! I feel sorry for them sometimes because they are destroying their own security.
(Paraphrase)

I am not able to talk with them anymore and avoid the topic of efficiency or effectiveness as much as I can. When they push me, however, I tell them just what I think, and then they really get angry. They can give criticism, but they can't take it. So I usually just withdraw into my own routine and let them wallow in the chaos. To hell with them! That's what I say. What do you say?

(Summarize)

Answer the following questions or discuss them with your partner.

1. Where did you mark in encouragers, and why?
2. Check your paraphrasing against the rules for Beta's culture to see if you were sensitive to it.
3. Check your summary against the rules for Beta's culture to see if you were sensitive to it.

THE GAMMA CLIENT

I am here on my own. Nobody knows that I have come here, and I will require you to keep this visit confidential. I presume that anything I say here will be kept private, between just you and me. That is our contract, and if you can't keep it let me know now so I can leave.
(Paraphrase)

My problem involves the people that work for and with me. They seem to have a hard time getting along with me, and I can't understand why. I certainly do my best to get along with them! They don't show me the respect they used to, so I don't respect them anymore either. It gets pretty tense around the place where we work, and that makes me uncomfortable.
(Paraphrase)

They insist on all these rules and regulations that are sometimes okay but generally just get in the way. I like to do my own thing and be left alone. That way I work best and have the highest production record of anybody. They can take all this other stuff and stick it you know where! Anyway, I don't like getting angry, and it's getting in the way of how I do my job, which is why I'm here talking with you.
(Paraphrase)

I might be wrong, you know. I might even be part of the problem, but if so I need to know so I can fix things. I keep wanting them to argue things out, but they run away from me when I do that. I'm tired of trying to help them run the place. There's nothing in it for me anymore. Feel how tense I am right here in my shoulders because of all this stress!

(Summarize)

Answer the following questions or discuss them with your partner.

1. Where did you mark in encouragers, and why?
2. Check your paraphrasing against the rules for Gamma's culture to see if you were sensitive to it.

3. Check your summary against the rules for Gamma's culture to see if you were sensitive to it.

THE DELTA CLIENT

Hi there! It's really great to see you! I've really been looking forward to spending some time with you here, if you know what I mean. It's a dog-eat-dog world out there, and I'm tired of eating dog all the time. I just want to get ahead with my career, you know? I want to make it, and time's a-wastin! You ever think about how short life is? Anyway, I'm working with a couple of screwups that are making my life hell.
(Paraphrase)

I know what I want, and I want you to help me get it. I've got the ball, and now I want to shoot and score! I deserve it. I've been doing most of the work around the place, while these goof-offs have been sitting on the bench. Don't get me wrong. I don't mind working hard. I like to make things work. Hey! I'm a team player, whatever they say. I'm no spoilsport. All I want is to kick a little ass or do whatever it takes to get these guys to do their part.
(Paraphrase)

I think the big problem is that I'm surrounded by a bunch of wusses. If I tell them what I think is wrong, they run like hell. How can you work with somebody if you can't disagree once in a while? Bunch of chickens. I think they're afraid of me now because I got kind of loud the other day. They told the boss on me, and he's the one that sent me to see you. He says he "cares," but I think he's just as chicken shit as they are.
(Paraphrase)

So . . . what should I do now? All the guys have their backs up against me. My boss thinks I'm a troublemaker. If I lose this job, I'm back out on the street, which is just not cool right now. I need a partner to win this game. That's clear. Hey! I'm ready to change if you can prove to me that I'm wrong. I've got no problem with that. Lay it on me!

(Summarize)

Answer the following questions or discuss them with your partner.

1. Where did you mark in encouragers, and why?
2. Check your paraphrasing against the rules for Delta's culture to see if you were sensitive to it.

3. Check your summary against the rules for Delta's culture to see if you were sensitive to it.

As you read over the four different presenting problems by Alpha, Beta, Gamma, and Delta, ask yourself with which cultures would you have done best, and with which ones would you have done worst? What parts of each culture did you see as similar to yourself? What parts of each culture did you see as different from yourself? Did you use the paraphrasing, summarizing, and encouraging skills differently with each culture? Look beyond the skill itself to the function it provides in each different cultural setting so that you can use it appropriately. It's important to recognize that these skills build on the feedback and attending skills of the previous chapters.

KEY IDEAS

1. The purpose of paraphrasing, summarizing, and encouraging.
   Help the interviewee feel more understood. Encourage the interviewee to contribute to the interview.
   Help clarify what has been said.
   Verify accuracy by checking out the interviewer's perception.
   Reduce the need for interviewees to repeat themselves.
   Increase the efficiency of the interview.
2. Paraphrasing skills.
   Provide the essence of what was said in the interviewer's own words.
   Include key words or phrases of special importance.
   Provide clarification where necessary to fill in gaps.
   Check out the accuracy of the paraphrase with the interviewee.
   Paraphrase with tone of voice and body language as well as words used.
3. Paraphrasing behaviors.
   Recall the interviewee's message to yourself.
   Identify the essence of that message.
   Translate that message into your own words.
   Check out the accuracy of your paraphrase.
4. Summarizing skills.
   Apply the same skills as for paraphrasing, but with more information.
   Usually used at the beginning or end of an interview.
   Useful for transition from one topic to another.
   May cover several interviews.
   Includes verbal and nonverbal messages.
5. Encourager skills.
   Includes head nods, gestures, saying of "um hmmm," and repetition of key words.
   Reassures the interviewee without interrupting the interview.

Silence can be an encourager.
Excessive use of encouragers can be annoying.
Encouragers should be natural and not forced.
6. Skill building.
Apply the rules of giving feedback.
Emphasize the importance of tracking, nonverbals, barriers, value assumptions, inferences, and discrepancies.

EXERCISE 6.5: PRACTICE IN USING PARAPHRASING, SUMMARIZING, AND ENCOURAGING SKILLS

In order to increase your ability to use paraphrasing, summarizing, and encouraging appropriately, follow these guidelines:

1. Select two partners to form a three-person group, with one person being the interviewer, one the interviewee, and one the observer.
2. Set up a ten-minute role-played interview, using synthetic cultures.
3. Follow up the role-played interview with a ten-minute discussion led by the observer, who will point out specific examples of paraphrasing, summarizing, and encouraging from written notes and specific examples.
4. Exchange roles so that each participant will have an opportunity to be the interviewer, interviewee, and observer. Remember also to use feedback skills and basic attending skills while you are learning paraphrasing, summarizing, and encouraging. Each unit of skills builds on the previous units.

Instructions to the observer: Listen and watch for specific examples of paraphrasing, summarizing, and encouraging skills used by the counselor.

1. Provided the essence of what was said in the interviewee's own words.
   Example:

2. Repeated key words or phrases of special importance.
   Example:

3. Checked out the accuracy of the paraphrase.
   Example:

4. Used nonverbals as well as verbals in paraphrasing.
   Example:

5. Used head nods and gestures to encourage.
   Example:

6. Used key words as encouragers.
   Example:

7. Used silence as an encourager.
   Example:

8. Did not use encouragers excessively.
   Example:

9. Encouragers were natural and not forced.
   Example:

10. Did not forget about feedback and attending skills.
    Example:

Chapter Seven

Question-Asking Skills

Major Objective:
To learn appropriate ways of obtaining accurate information from culturally different clients.

Secondary Objectives:
1. To learn and practice the various uses of question asking with culturally different clients.
2. To review the various functions and levels of complexity in different types of questions.
3. To practice asking ethnographic questions with the four synthetic cultures.

Questions are the most frequently used—and overused—tool of interviewers and counselors. Questions can be used to encourage or discourage talking. Usually the questions are asked by the interviewer and answered by the interviewee, putting the interviewer in control of the situation. Questions have a great deal to do with power. When counselors lose control in an interview, they sometimes ask a new question as the means of recapturing control. Question-asking skills increase a counselor's ability to collect specific information, redirect the interview, or encourage the interviewee to disclose general information.

Questions help the interviewer understand specific details about the interviewee in order to make appropriate decisions based on accurate information. They can control the quantity and quality of information in the interview. Open questions such as "What do you think about that?" tend to encourage the interviewee to speak more. Closed questions tend to be more specific and require only one or two word answers, such as "Will you come here tomorrow?" A skilled interviewer will know when and how to use both open and closed questions.

1. Open questions help begin an interview.
2. Open questions elaborate and enrich the interview.
3. Closed questions keep the interview from wandering off track.
4. Closed questions fill in specific information gaps.

THE FUNCTION OF QUESTIONS

There are several functions of questions in the counseling interview. They may be used to:

1. Identify specific facts about the client.
2. Identify problems, concerns, or issues for the client.
3. Clarify specific details.
4. Get facts with questions beginning with "what."
5. Reveal feelings or processes with questions beginning with "how."
6. Get at motives with questions beginning with "why."

There are several problems with using questions—and especially with overusing questions—in counseling.

1. The feeling of bombardment or grilling results from asking too many questions. In some cultures questions can be seen as rude and intrusive.
2. When multiple questions are asked at the same time, it is hard to know which to answer.
3. When questions are used rhetorically, they are not really questions at all.
4. When questions are culturally insensitive, they will offend culturally different people.
5. Questions that begin with "why" may be intrusive and offend the inter-viewee.

Some interviews are nothing more than a question/answer session where the interviewer never gives up control. The interviewee just waits for the interviewer to go on to the next topic and passively follows. Other interviews try not to use any questions, which places much more responsibility for the discussion on the interviewee. The nonuse of questions is also an important question-asking skill.

There are at least seven basic kinds of questions, ranging from the simplest and most elementary to the most complicated (Sanders, 1966). Let us examine each progressively, from the least to the most complicated.

1. Memory questions require the recall or recognition of information and are the least complicated. ("What happened?")

2. Translation questions change information into symbols or language. An idea or thought is restated using different words. ("Is there another way of saying that?")

3. Interpretation questions identify and select appropriate generalizations. ("What did he mean when he said that?")

4. Application questions identify and select appropriate generalizations. ("What have you learned from what he meant?")

5. Analysis questions solve problems through conscious knowledge and thinking. ("What have you learned from that situation that will help you in other situations?")

6. Synthesis questions solve problems with original thinking. ("What are some ways of dealing with this situation you haven't yet tried?")

7. Evaluation questions make judgments of good or bad according to standards and are the most complicated. ("Which way do you think works best?")

Good counseling will use the full range of question types and not limit questions to mere tests of memory. By going beyond memory questions, the client's critical thinking ability can be encouraged. Each different kind of question leads to a different line of thinking. The more complicated questions give the client some credit for bringing resources into the interview. A really good question will have no simple answer but will encourage a great deal of constructive exploration. Each of the seven categories of questions has unique elements but also includes some element of all lower categories, so that evaluation questions build on all six easier types of questions. Memory is part of every kind of question. To test your ability to classify questions, identify one example of each of the seven kinds of questions regarding the same basic problem, and ask your partner to verify that your examples are accurate.

THE PURPOSE OF ASKING QUESTIONS

The different theoretical perspectives of counseling advocate the use of questions in different ways. Ellis (1977) suggests that rational-emotive therapy take a Socratic questioning stance, rather than make declarative statements. The rational-emotive therapist is likely to use direct, closed questions about cognition (ideas) the client has. Rogers (1951), on the other hand, recommends that questions not be used at all; counselors should rely exclusively on declarative statements. In the rare instance when a nondirective therapist would use questions, the question would be indirect, open, and probably about feelings. Other more eclectic theoretical orientations take their own perspective on when and how to use questions. The cognitive behavioral and psychodynamic traditions use questions extensively. If the focus is on the client and the counselor is culturally sensitive, questions are a very valuable tool.

In some styles of therapy the client is discouraged from asking questions, and in the rare instance where a client asks a question, the counselor is encouraged not to answer it. The rationale is usually that client questions might foster dependency on the therapist or detract from self-examination. A therapist might therefore respond to a client's question—or the feeling/motive behind it—but not answer it. A further rationale is that self-enquiry is encouraged by not answering clients' questions, so that they can eventually answer their own.

In every instance it would be useful, as Dillon (1990) points out, to consider three issues about your use of questions in every counseling interview:

1. What was the purpose of the question(s)?
2. How was that purpose therapeutic?
3. To what extent did the question(s) achieve that purpose?

Ivey (1991) discusses the use of questioning at five different developmental stages for a client. Each stage of client development would indicate a different kind of question to accomplish a different purpose.

At the opening presentation of an issue, the counselor might ask a very general question like "What would you like to talk about today?" The purpose would be to get the client to provide background in a presenting problem. The counselor would use paraphrasing and encouragers to urge the client along with as little interruption as possible, then summarize the most important elements.

At what Ivey calls the "sensorimotor/elemental" next level, the counselor would try to understand how a client organizes the world, looking specifically at visual, auditory, and kinesthetic perceptions of the client in ways that make the problem concrete, rather than abstract. The counselor would help the client identify patterns and make sense out of the situation.

At the concrete-operational/situational third level, the counselor uses questions to collect facts in a linear description of events, with little emphasis on feelings or evaluation. The counselor will help the client describe what happened before and after the problem, but will not interpret the situation. The counselor uses questions to get the client thinking about the problem.

At the formal operational pattern fourth level, the counselor gets clients talking about themselves and repeated patterns, going beyond description to analysis and interpretation. Abstract thinking about problems is encouraged, and problems are seen within a larger context from multiple perspectives.

At the dialectic/systemic/integrative fifth level the counselor integrates insights from all previous levels to help the client see how he or she constructed the problem, recognize different perspectives about it, and help construct a solution. The client is encouraged to challenge assumptions and take control of the situation.

Counselors are provided with alternative perspectives to help them decide how questions might best be used. This is particularly true when the counselor is working in a multicultural environment where there are culturally learned assumptions implicit both in the way a question is asked and the way in which that same question is understood.

Consider, for example, questions that might be acceptable or unacceptable to clients in each of the four synthetic cultures. Identify the purpose of the question, the therapeutic contribution (if any), and the extent to which each question accomplished that therapeutic purpose. Refer to the guidelines and rules for each of the cultures to judge appropriateness.

Clients from any culture change and develop over time. The potential for them becoming better or worse is always there. Questions appropriate at one stage of development might not be at another stage. In multicultural counseling, however, the rules and guidelines that define the different stages will be different. The multicultural counselor will still have to match each question with the appropriate level (high/low, strong/weak, complex/simple) for the client and be willing to adjust the level of questions as the client changes. Ivey, Ivey, and Simek-Morgan (1993) developed a stage structure for measuring development in counseling that moves from the generally simple to a more complex understanding of a client's situation. This structure has been adapted below to the four synthetic cultures.

QUESTIONING SEQUENCE

Opening Presentation of Issue

Alpha. Begin with a polite prelude that establishes the relationship, rather than move directly to the task. Be sensitive to the client's bringing up possible questions directly or indirectly, then follow up with an opening question, like: "Can you tell me what you would like to talk about today?"

Beta. Begin by developing an agenda or a structure that will diminish uncertainty and define (at least temporarily) what will be covered in the interview, like: "Can you identify two or three topics you would like us to focus on today?"

Gamma. Begin by focusing directly on the individual's needs and purpose in coming to the counseling session, like: "Can you tell me what would be most helpful to you in our session today?"

Delta. Begin by focusing on the utility of the session and the way this session will help the client be more successful, like: "Can you tell me what would be most useful to you in our session today?"

Goal. Obtain a story of from fifty to one hundred words. Assess overall functioning of the client on varying cognitive-development levels as appropriate to the client's cultural background. Use questions, encouragers, paraphrasing, and reflection of feeling to bring out data, but try to impact or interrupt the client as little as possible. Get the story as he or she constructs it. Summarize key facts and feelings about what the client has said before moving on.

Sensorimotor/Elemental

This stage of the questioning sequence assumes that a very solid basis of trust has been established and you are now ready to get into the client's deeper emotions.

Alpha. Focus on the traditional feelings that the hierarchy will expect or impose on the client and how the client may be embarrassed by not being comfortable with those required emotions, like: "What are the feelings you are supposed to have in your situation?"

Beta. Be formal and unambiguous in separating good from bad feelings by describing specific emotions directly, like: "What are the three most important emotions you experience in that situation?"

Gamma. Personalize your description of emotions and focus on the unique feelings of that particular individual, like: "How are your feelings different from other people's around you?"

Delta. Focus on how emotions help or hinder the individual's success and progress, like: "What are the ways your emotions help you or get in your way?"

Goal. Elicit one example, then explore what was seen, heard, or felt. Aim for here-and-now experiencing of emotions. Recognize that descriptions of emotions might ramble and seem random in their direction. Summarize at the end of the segment. You might want to ask yourself: "What one emotion or feeling stands out for the client from all this?"

Concrete/Situational

Alpha. Be sensitive to the hierarchy of power and authority, which might constrain the client and require more indirect or subtle communication of problems, like: "What would I notice, as an outsider, if I were to visit you in your own community?"

Beta. Be sensitive to the need for specific detail, structured format, and unambiguous language, like: "Could you give me three specific examples of the situation/issue/problem?"

Gamma. Be sensitive to the role and relative importance of the individual in society, like: "Can you describe your feelings in the situation and how you would like things to be?"

Delta. Be sensitive to the need to succeed and assert a point of view, whatever the risk, like: "What things get in your way and prevent you from being more successful?"

Goal. Obtain a linear description of the event. Look for examples of reasoning from specific causes to specific effects. Ask yourself: "What did he or she do? Say? What happened before? What happened next? What happened after? What are the consequences of each thing he or she did?" Summarize what you learned before moving on. Focus on feelings as well as facts to integrate both the cognitive-thinking and the affective-feeling messages the client is sending.

Formal/Pattern

Alpha. Be sensitive to traditional patterns that control the client's behavior and how comfortable the client may be with those expectations, like: "Do others expect you always to behave in the same way, or do you sometimes behave differently?"

Beta. Identify the rules and laws that define patterns in the client's life and which provide a certain order, like: "What are three basic principles that guide you in deciding what to do?"

Gamma. Recognize the almost chaotic and spontaneous way of making decisions according to short-term goals, like: "What is the best thing that can happen, from your own point of view?"

Delta. Be goal directed in describing the patterns that would be most likely to succeed, like: "What game plan would you use to win in this situation?"

Goal. Talk about repeating patterns and situations that are important from the client's viewpoint. Ask yourself: "What was the client saying to herself or himself when that happened? Has the client felt like that in other situations?" Reflect on feelings, and paraphrase as appropriate. Summarize carefully the key facts and feelings you learned before moving on.

Dialectic/Systematic/Integrative

Begin by summarizing to yourself all that has been said. Ask yourself: "How does the client put together or organize all that he or she told me? What one thing stands out most for the client? How many different ways can the client describe his or her feelings and how they change?"

Alpha. Recognize the importance of the client's social context and the hierarchy of authority to which the client is expected to conform. Encourage the client to describe this context, like: "What do your leaders want you to do in this situation?"

Beta. Recognize the need for answers and solutions in specific, rather than general, terms for solving problems and resolving conflict, like: "What are the rules you will use to guide your decisions in the future?"

Gamma. Focus on the very complex and even apparently disordered need to keep all options open and for self-protection in all situations, like: "Can you describe your strengths and weaknesses to me?"

Delta. Focus on the competitive and achievement orientation of the client to succeed, however difficult that might be, like: "What are the things you will have to do now to succeed later?"

Goals. (1) To obtain an integrated summary of what has been said; (2) to enable the client to see how reality is co-constructed, not developed from a single view; (3) to obtain different perspectives on the same situation and be aware that each is just one perspective; (4) to note flaws in the present construction, co-construction, or perspective, and move to action.

As we move toward more complex reasoning, several options are open. Before using any of them, summarize to yourself and later to the client what the client has been saying over the entire series of questions.

Integration: How do you put together or organize all that the client told you? What one thing stands out most?

Co-construction: What rule was the client operating under? Where did that rule come from? How might someone else (perhaps another family member) describe the situation? Feelings can be examined using the same questions.

Multiple perspectives: How could we describe this from the point of view of some other person or using another theoretical framework or language system? How else might we put it together using another framework?

Deconstruction and action: Can you see some flaws in the reasoning or in the patterns of feelings above? How might the client change the rules? Given these possibilities, what action might the client take?

In working with synthetic culture simulation in the past, I have discovered that the actual content of the question is much less important than the words you use. Each culture has some words that result in a positive reaction and some that result in a negative reaction. As you put together your question, focus not only on the function of the question but also on the actual words you use.

QUESTIONING FOR SYNTHETIC CULTURES

Questioning the Alpha Client

In questioning the Alpha client it will be important to keep in mind the importance of respect, the vertical ordering of authority in which the client has found a place, the importance of wisdom and insight, the willingness to obey orders and to please authority figures. It is also useful to remember that when Alphas ask for help they are showing their trust in you. Alphas will be formal and will expect you to be formal also. Alphas will tend to blame themselves as a form of politeness and to avoid conflict.

Imagine you have an Alpha client whom you believe to be lonely and isolated. What are some of the questions you might ask?

1.

2.

3.

4.

Questioning the Beta Client

In questioning the Beta client you should be as structured, organized, and unambiguous as possible. Betas will respond positively to the discovery of truth as a goal of questioning. Your questions will be helpful if they lead to clear and certain solutions or approaches. Betas like to be taught something they already know; it reaffirms their understanding. They will respond positively to a predictable line of questioning. Never surprise a Beta! If you go on a "fishing expedition" questioning a Beta, you will get very negative results. Do your homework and know where you are going. Betas will be intolerant of silly or frivolous questions. They will answer your questions directly and in detail if they feel positively toward you. Don't be surprised if a Beta puts a value judgment on what you are saying, and don't be surprised if a Beta client asks you questions back. You might well feel intimidated by your Beta client. You won't change a Beta's mind, but you might help restructure the situation in a way that will help the client see things differently.

Imagine you have a Beta client whom you believe to be lonely and isolated. What are some of the questions you might ask?

1.

2.

3.

4.

Questioning the Gamma Client

In questioning the Gamma client you are dealing with an individual who likes being emotionally independent. The Gamma will use friendships but is mostly self-reliant and believes that if everybody would only take care of themselves, the world would be a better place. Questions challenging that independence will be threatening. Questions that help the person find ways to self-improvement will be welcome. Gammas are very protective of their dignity and don't like embarrassing questions. They like to explore new ideas and alternatives, and they like a new, exciting challenge. Pitch your question toward the explorer in the Gamma, and even high-risk questions will become acceptable. However, any question that might humiliate the Gamma will get you nowhere. Remember, they make their own rules, so even implicit criticism of them for not following rules will be a sensitive area. Gammas don't mind self-disclosing, on their own terms. They love a debate or argument, and taking you on shows that they trust you. Gammas are likely to ask you some hard questions also and will be sensitive to your own defensiveness or insecurity as a sign of weakness.

Imagine you have a Gamma client whom you believe to be lonely and isolated. What are some of the questions you might ask?

1.

2.

3.

4.

Questioning the Delta Client

Your Delta client is assertive and even aggressive in responding to your questions, so you can expect a lively, rough-and-tumble interview. Deltas like to compete, so don't be surprised if your Delta client challenges you from time to time. The interview might resemble a game where you and the client serve questions back and forth like a Ping-Pong ball. The Delta client will respect a good, penetrating question just like a hard serve, and even a question with some spin on it will be appreciated as a sign of your skill. You need to think quickly to stay ahead of your Delta client, and getting distracted or losing concentration will not be helpful. The Delta client will accept the most awkward or sensitive question as long as you are not self-conscious asking it. On the other hand, you can expect Delta clients to "take no prisoners" if you lose their respect. Deltas like a good discussion with lively interchange, so controversial or provocative questions might be appropriate. The Delta client will take you on to see how good you are before trusting you. Be ready for an argument. Don't get into a fault-finding sequence of questions that tries to fix blame. Emphasize style and repartee. Even joking might be appropriate—although that's always risky.

Imagine you have a Delta client whom you believe to be lonely and isolated. What are some of the questions you might ask?

1.

2.

3.

4.

THE ETHNOGRAPHIC QUESTION

Practicing question building for each of the four synthetic cultures should help you identify a range of different questions that might be appropriate to get at the same problem across different cultures. There is a rich literature on the use of questions in multicultural situations under the heading of "ethnographic methodology." This means of gathering information was developed by anthropologists in the last century; only recently has it been applied to counseling (Wehrly and Watson-Gegeo, 1985). In part, this development has resulted from a disappointment by multicultural counselors in the more objective methods of gathering information as inappropriate. The ethnographic interview tries to describe or get at the "way of living" in a culture or group, looking for patterns of behavior and shared meaning.

The ethnographer will try to describe and interpret the information gathered from the client's own point of view, rather than from the more universal viewpoint of abstract theories. The interviewer looks at relationships, patterns, and processes both within and across cultures. The ethnographer usually spends considerable amounts of time in the host culture as a participant observer. Ethnographic questions allow us to step outside our own culture and examine a contrasting set of assumptions, seeing the world from another viewpoint. As you consider questions, add the question "why?" to each. Go beyond the outward manifestation of the culture to an understanding of why some patterns prevail and their underlying values. In some cases, you would not actually ask ethnographic questions, but you might discover answers by observing or listening carefully.

Spradley (1976) defines culture as the acquired knowledge that people use to interpret experience and generate social behavior. It is the knowledge for acting, believing, perceiving, and feeling. He describes the process of ethnographic interviewing and more specifically how to ask ethnographic questions to understand someone else's culture better. In order to ask good ethnographic questions, it is first useful to discover the right questions to ask. You can discover these by (1) listening to children ask parents; (2) listening to students ask teachers; (3) listening to daily conversations, or (4) just listening for patterns in the other culture.

There are several different types of ethnographic questions. The first are descriptive. (1) There is the typical "grand tour" question, like: "Could you describe a typical day?"; or the specific grand tour question, like: "Could you describe yesterday?"; or the guided grand tour question, like: "Could you show me around?"; or the task-related grand tour question, like: "Could you draw a map of this place?" (2) There is the typical mini-tour question, like: "Could you tell me about a typical phone call?"; or the specific mini-tour question, like: "Could you describe several phone calls you had today?"; or the guided mini-tour question, like: "Could you show me how you organize your desk?"; or the task-related mini-tour question, like: "Could you draw a chart showing how things are organized?" (3) There are example questions, like: "Could you give me an example of being chewed out?" (4) There are experience questions, like: "Could you tell me some experiences you have had with obnoxious people?" (5) There are open-ended descriptive questions, like: "Could you tell me about yourself?" (6) There are native language questions that may be direct, like: "What would you use for this?"; or typical, like: "What would he say?" You might prepare descriptive questions by going through an imaginary interview, writing down questions in combination with other elements of the interview beforehand to increase verbal output or recall, to expand on explanations, to encourage restatements.

The second type of ethnographic questions are structural to discover cultural domains, the members of the domains, and their primary organization. A cultural domain is a folk or analytic concept subsystem of a group's cultural knowledge shared by group members and organized. There are several ways that questions help you identify structure. (1) Cover term questions move from the general to the specific, like: "What are all the different things you do here?" (2) Member term questions move from the specific to the general, like: "Is this typewriter a kind of something?" (3) Substitution frame questions are like: "I think that _____ is busy work. Can you fill in words that might fit here?" (4) Card-sorting structural questions ask the person to organize, like: "You do many things. Could you sort them into groups or bunches that fit together?" (5) Verification questions ask for proof, like: "Is making coffee a kind of work?" In asking structural questions you would first explain the question, using native language as much as possible, and restate the other person's responses to check accuracy. It is useful to distinguish between personal and cultural information questions. A personal question would be, "What do you do?" A cultural approach would ask what most people do.

A third type of ethnographic question focuses on contrasting the attributes or meanings of each term inside a cultural domain. There are several that focus on differences among concepts. (1) An unrestricted contrast describes permanent differences, like: "Are these always different from those?" (2) A restricted contrast describes temporary differences, like: "When might these two go together?" (3) A question might clarify contrasting cultural domains. (4) A question might clarify contrasting taxonomies for organizing information. (5) A question might explore differences in meaning. Contrast questions might clarify differences among two, three, or more concepts, asking the other person directly or indirectly by rating or ranking them.

THE PROCESS OF QUESTION ASKING

The way a question is worded will influence the answer you get. In popularity polls and in some research, questions are slanted to get desired information. There is an implicit answer built into each question. This danger is especially serious in asking questions across cultures. There are several ways you can minimize this source of error in formulating your questions (Segall, 1986).

1. Keep the question concrete and specific. The less ambiguous the question, the easier it will be to interpret the answer accurately. It is possible to be concrete and specific even when asking for an opinion.

2. Be careful about how the question is worded. Try to make sure that it is understood as it was intended. The words used should be familiar, and the sentence structure should be clear. At the same time, the question should not indicate a preferred answer, or it will become rhetorical. You want the other person's answer to your question. It might be a good idea to pretest some questions with persons from your client's culture ahead of time to discover any possible problems. Questions never work in another culture in totally predictable ways.

3. Ask your questions in the right order. You might, for example, begin with more specific questions and then move toward the more general. In any case, think through the sequence you will use.

4. Be especially careful of the language you use in your questions. It is best if the question can be asked in the client's own first language or language of choice. Working through a translator is especially difficult and raises a whole range of new issues and problems.

Cormier and Cormier (1991) discuss questions under the section on "action responses" by counselors in interviews. The purpose of action responses according to them and to Egan (1990) is for clients to discover the need to change in an action-oriented, objective frame of reference. These action responses—such as questions—are always and necessarily based on careful listening and reflect the counselor's understanding of the client. The open question or probe is a tool that is useful to begin the interview, to encourage client elaboration/information disclosure, to elicit specific examples of client behaviors/feelings/thoughts, and to motivate the client to communicate more. The closed question is useful to narrow the topic of discussion, to get specific information, to define the boundaries of a problem, to restrain over-talkative clients, and to focus the counseling session. Cormier and Cormier suggest five guidelines in the use of probes or questions.

1. The question must focus on the client's concerns and not the counselor's curiosity or need for closure.
2. A pause after the question will give the client time to respond. The client may not have a quick answer to your question.
3. Ask only one question at a time. Asking multiple questions is confusing to both the client and counselor.
4. Avoid accusing or antagonizing the client unnecessarily. The accusation may be either intentional or unintentional and might be conveyed by voice tone, nonverbal language, or the verbal message.
5. Don't rely on questions as the primary response mode in an interview, except in an intake or a pure information-gathering interview.

KEY IDEAS

1. The purpose of question-asking skills.
   To encourage or discourage talking.
   To put the interviewer back in control of the interview.
   To encourage the interviewee to disclose information.
2. Open question skills.
   Help to begin an interview.
   Elaborate and enrich the interview.
   Encourage otherwise silent clients to talk.
3. Closed question skills.
   Keep the interview from wandering off-topic.
   Fill in specific information gaps.
   Slow down clients that are otherwise too talkative.
4. Functions of questioning.
   Identify specific facts.
   Identify problems, concerns, or issues.
   Clarify details.
5. Misuse of questioning skills.
   Bombardment or grilling by asking too many questions.
   Asking more than one question at the same time.
   Using questions rhetorically.
   Using culturally insensitive questions.
6. Types of questions.
   Memory to test recall or recognition.
   Translation to change information into symbols.
   Interpretation to discover relationships among symbols.

Application to apply symbols appropriately.
Analysis to solve problems using symbols.
Synthesis to solve problems with original thinking.
Evaluation to judge goodness or badness.

7. The purpose of asking questions.
Some theoretical orientations prescribe the use of questions more than others.
Questions to begin an interview focus on establishing a relationship.
Questions appropriate to the sensorimotor/elemental stages look at the client's organization of reality.
Questions appropriate to the concrete/operational/situational level are to collect facts.
Questions appropriate to the formal/operational level look for repeated patterns.
Questions appropriate to the dialectic/systematic/integrative level develop new and creative insights.
Each synthetic culture has a different emphasis in asking appropriate questions at each level.

8. Questions for synthetic cultures.
Questioning the Alpha client: Emphasize respect and hierarchical authority.
Questioning the Beta client: Emphasize unambiguous structure and organization.
Questioning the Gamma client: Emphasize individualism and emotional independence.
Questioning the Delta client: Emphasize success and the achievement of goals.

9. The ethnographic question.
Questions must be sensitive to their cultural context.
Descriptive questions are often used first.
Structural questions are used to discover cultural domains.
Attribute- or meaning-oriented questions explore the cultural domain.

10. The process of question asking.
Keep questions specific.
Be careful of wording.
Ask questions in the right order.
Be careful of the language you use.
Focus on the client's concerns.
Pause after your questions.
Ask only one question at a time.
Avoid accusing or antagonizing the client.
Don't over-rely on questions for getting information.

EXERCISE 7.1: QUESTION-ASKING SKILLS

In order to practice your use of questions in the interview, role-play a ten-minute interview with your partner and an observer to exchange feedback. Follow these steps:

1. Organize into a three-person group with one person being the interviewee, one the interviewer, and one the observer. The person in the interviewee role will take on the identity of a synthetic culture (Alpha, Beta, Gamma, or Delta) of his or her choice.
2. Select a topic and role-play an interview, with the observer taking notes on specific questions asked by the interviewer.
3. After the interview the observer will lead a discussion from notes identifying specific questions that were asked. Feedback will be provided to the interviewer about how questions might have been used differently.
4. The partners will exchange roles until each has experienced all three. The observer should think of him- or herself as a teacher, remembering the rules for giving feedback, with the goal of increasing the skill of the interviewer in a facilitative way.

Instructions to the observer: Listen and watch for specific examples of questioning skills as they are used in the interview.

1. Were open questions used near the beginning of the interview?
   Example:

2. Were open questions used to elaborate and enrich the interview?
   Example:

3. Were open questions used to encourage otherwise silent clients to talk?
   Example:

4. Were closed questions used to keep the interview from wandering off-topic?
   Example:

5. Were closed questions used to fill in specific information gaps?
   Example:

6. Were closed questions used to slow down the client when he or she became too talkative?
   Example:

7. Did the counselor bombard or grill the client by asking too many questions?
   Example:

8. Did the counselor ask more than one question at the same time?
   Example:

9. Did the counselor use questions rhetorically?
   Example:

10. Did the counselor use culturally insensitive questions?
    Example:

11. Did the client ask questions at the appropriate developmental level for the client's culture?
    Example:

Chapter Eight

Reflecting Feeling and Reflecting Meaning

Major Objective:
To reflect and interpret accurately the feelings and meanings of a culturally different client.

Secondary Objectives:
1. To identify and confirm the feelings of a culturally different client accurately.
2. To identify and confirm the intentional meanings conveyed by a culturally different client accurately.
3. To identify how empathy incorporates the accurate identification of feelings and meanings.

Although most of the books on counselor skill training separate reflections of feelings from reflections of meaning, this chapter will deal with them as symbiotic, or interrelated. Feelings relate to the affective and frequently more explicit, observable, and emotional aspects of a problem. Meanings relate to the cognitive and usually more implicit, hidden, and more intellectual aspects of a problem. Culture-centered counseling must not only separate feelings from meanings to deal with them separately but must also unite them through empathy to see how they each contribute to the organic life of problems in counseling.

REFLECTION OF FEELINGS

Reflecting feelings is the process of making the implicit more explicit. Reflection of feelings is accomplished by giving feedback on which feelings are being displayed in the interview, whether or not they were intended.

Reflection of feelings helps clarify and focus the interview. Each of us has preferred words that exactly describe and focus the feelings we experience. It is useful to identify and perhaps expand that pool of feeling words.

Identify at least ten different synonyms for each of the following ten adjectives describing a range of emotions.

1. Love

2. Happiness

3. Fear

4. Anger

5. Contempt

6. Mirth

7. Surprise

8. Suffering

9. Determination

10. Disgust

If you can find a letter that you have written to a friend, go through it and underline all the words describing an emotion or a feeling. You will probably find that you use a relatively small variety of emotion or feeling words. Reflection of feelings also incorporates the basic attending skills, paraphrasing, encouraging, summarizing, questioning, and feedback discussed earlier.

Frequently persons have mixed feelings and are not sure themselves about what they feel. This confusion can interfere with an interview unless the feelings are clarified. Running away from mixed feelings is usually not the best solution for either the interviewee or the interviewer. This confusion is particularly a problem when the client and counselor come from different cultures.

Sometimes the interviewer will infer certain feelings, but unless that inference is checked out, the interviewer may be wrong and never realize it. Timing is very important when dealing with feelings. After making a tentative statement about the interviewee's feelings, it is important to immediately check out whether that feeling was accurately identified. If the reflection of feelings skill is used too much, however, it can also destroy the interview, so it must be used carefully.

EXERCISE 8.1: NESTED FEELINGS

In reflecting, note (1) the specifically expressed emotional words used by a client; (2) the implicit emotional words not actually spoken; (3) nonverbally expressed emotions; and (4) mixed and often discrepant verbal/nonverbal emotional cues.

Not everyone will welcome your interpretation of their feelings. Sometimes the use of metaphors is helpful in discussing feelings.

The following exercise will help you evaluate your own ability to identify feelings accurately.

1. Request a culturally different volunteer to talk for three or four minutes about a situation experienced that resulted in strong (positive or negative or mixed) feelings.

2. The other participants will listen carefully to the volunteer's story and the feelings displayed.

3. All participants (including the storyteller) will score the extent to which the storyteller experienced the following feelings both at the time of the event and as telling the story. A 10 (high score) indicates a great deal of feeling. A 1 (low score) indicates very little or no feeling.

Feeling	Then	Now
Love		
Happiness		
Fear		
Anger		
Contempt		
Mirth		
Surprise		
Suffering		
Determination		
Disgust		

4. The storyteller will read his or her score on all ten feelings, and the other participants will score their answers in terms of how accurately they were able to identify the stated feelings.

Other theoretical perspectives deal with the reflection of feelings in a variety of different ways (Corey, 1991). Adlerian therapists do not focus directly on feelings, but rather on the beliefs that led to those feelings. Feelings are the result of, rather than the cause of, thoughts and beliefs. Feelings result from the way a person thinks and lead to the way the person acts. Adlerians would approach feelings through the clients' thoughts.

Behaviorism also deemphasizes feelings or emotional processes, assuming that feelings follow behaviors, and if the counselor can change the behaviors the feelings will follow. In their discussion of empathy Kanfer and Goldstein

(1986) indicate that affective dimensions in behavioral therapy are important in modifying cognitive and behavioral events.

The existentialists view feelings as facilitative, helping put the client in touch with reality. Feelings such as anxiety, for example, can motivate the client to change. The existentialist counselor might help a client become one with her or his feelings. Normal anxiety is a part of life and should not be eliminated. Feelings would be reflected as a friendly resource of energy for change.

Rational-emotive therapy helps clients eliminate their irrational feelings. They are reflected back to put the client in control of which feelings they want to increase or decrease. The counselor works as a teacher to help clients learn ways to take control of their feelings and change their lives through more rational thinking.

Person-centered approaches to therapy help the client explore a wider range of feelings to accept and explore them. The first stage of therapy is helping the client identify, explore, and express feelings in a safe setting. Clients have the right and the ability to discover their own feelings, and the counselor's task is to provide a facilitative relationship.

The psychoanalytic perspective sees feelings as symbolic of deeper thoughts, beliefs, and ideas that control the client. The feelings are a resource or pathway to understanding the client better. The client is encouraged to transfer feelings about others to the counselor so that the feelings can be made more conscious. The feelings themselves are less important than the state of mind they symbolize.

Reality therapy deals with the whole person, helping him or her get what he or she wants by negotiating goals within the constraints of reality. The counselor functions as a teacher, leading the client to insights about how actions and thoughts can control feelings, rather than be controlled by feelings. The counselor works with clients by first establishing a relationship of trust and a supportive relationship wherein reflection of feelings would be a useful skill.

Cormier and Cormier (1991) separate client statements expressing content or cognition—referring to people, events, situations, or ideas—from messages expressing feelings verbally or nonverbally about the content expressing the client's affective response. They contend that affect and cognition are combined in client messages, and it is useful to separate them so they can be treated differently. The reflection of feeling is used to rephrase affective messages, adding an emotional component to the paraphrased content. They discuss five purposes of reflecting feeling.

1. Reflecting feeling helps clients feel understood and will facilitate their communication with the counselor.

2. Reflection helps clients express more of their positive and negative feelings in safety, and becomes the means toward more important counseling goals.

3. Reflection helps clients take control of and manage feelings.

4. Reflecting a client's negative feelings about counseling or the counselor helps the client take risks in safety and may reduce nonproductive anger or strong feelings on other client topics.

5. Reflecting helps clients discriminate and distinguish between mixed feelings and become more specific in identifying and labeling feelings.

Cormier and Cormier describe five steps for learning how to reflect feelings, identify the emotional tone of an interview, and rephrase the client's feelings in an articulate way.

1. The first step is to listen for feeling or affect words in what the client says, expressing anger, fear, uncertainty, sadness, happiness, strength, or weakness. Feelings might also be revealed through nonverbal behaviors.

2. The second step is to reflect the feelings back to the client in your own words. The words need to reflect the feeling and intensity, requiring counselors to develop a large repertoire of words on which they can draw.

3. The third step is to take a basic sentence stem that may be visual ("It looks like . . ."), auditory ("It sounds like . . ."), or kinesthetic ("It feels like . . .")—whichever best reflects the way that client would talk.

4. The fourth step is to add on the situation in which the feelings occurred, which puts the feeling in a specific context, thereby reflecting your awareness of when and why those feelings occurred as well as the feelings themselves.

5. The fifth step is to check how effective you were and to verify the accuracy of your reflection of feeling.

Brammer (1988) adds the caution that a counselor should be particularly careful about encouraging emotional expression when:

1. The client has a severe emotional disorder.

2. Clients are under such pressure that they may respond with more intensity than they can control.

3. The client has a history of emotional crises getting out of hand.

4. The client is strongly and explicitly against exploring feelings.

5. The counselor is not sure how to help people deal with their feelings.

Another factor to consider is the counselor's own feelings, which might facilitate or get in the way of counseling. Having feelings is normal, as long as the counselor is able to monitor those feelings so that they don't distort the counseling message. It is useful for the counselor to listen and self-interpret what he or she is saying. The same skills used to detect client feelings can also help detect the counselor's own. Look for discrepancies, changes in topic, changes in body language, distractions, and other danger signs. Sometimes self-disclosure of your own feelings can be helpful as a model of risk-taking, but in other cultures it destroys your credibility completely.

It may be useful to practice reflection of feeling with each of the four synthetic cultures. This will help you develop more than one way of reflecting feelings according to the constraints and opportunities of your client's culture.

EXERCISE 8.2: REFLECTING FEELINGS IN SYNTHETIC CULTURES

Words describing feelings characteristic of each synthetic culture will be provided below. Imagine that you are working with a client from that culture and you have now become convinced that the client is experiencing that feeling with regard to family issues. Write down a statement showing reflection of feelings (ROF) for each of the four synthetic cultures when a member of that culture seems to be showing unfriendliness, distrust, or boredom.

Alpha Client Feelings

1. Unfriendliness: Alphas show friendliness by being soft-spoken and polite and listening, while they will show unfriendliness by being quiet and polite and not listening.
   ROF:

2. Distrust: Alphas show trust by asking for help and direction, while they will show distrust by not asking for help or direction.
   ROF:

3. Boredom: Alphas show interest through positive nonverbals, while they show boredom by being expressionless and unanimated.
   ROF:

Beta Client Feelings

1. Unfriendliness: Betas show unfriendliness through casual, general, and ambiguous responses.
   ROF:

2. Distrust: Betas show trust in their polarized structures, unambiguously separat-

ing right from wrong, while they will distrust by being openly critical and challenging the other person's credentials.
ROF:

3. Boredom: Betas show interest by actively asking task-oriented questions and maintaining direct eye contact, while they show boredom by being passive, quiet, and avoiding direct eye contact.
ROF:

Gamma Client Feelings

1. Unfriendliness: Gammas show friendliness by being verbal and self-disclosing, while they show unfriendliness by criticizing others behind their backs and sabotaging their enemies.
ROF:

2. Distrust: Gammas show trust by aggressively debating issues and actively controlling an interview, while they show distrust by being noncommittal on issues, passive, ambiguous, or even defensive.
ROF:

3. Boredom: Gammas show interest by being loudly verbal, asking lots of questions and seeking close physical contact, while they show boredom by maintaining a physical distance with no questions or eye contact.
ROF:

Delta Client Feelings

1. Unfriendliness: Deltas show friendliness by seeking physical contact and being loud and somewhat seductive, while they show unfriendliness by maintaining a physical distance and being sarcastic or even sadistic.
ROF:

2. Distrust: Deltas show trust by being competitive and seeking to dominate a discussion, while they show distrust by being openly critical and disparaging and attempting to end a discussion.
ROF:

3. Boredom: Deltas show interest by being eager to debate every issue from all points of view like a sports event, while they show boredom by avoiding direct eye contact and being discourteous and even drowsy.
ROF:

Examine the rules for the four synthetic cultures and the procedures for reflecting feeling in this chapter to evaluate your responses. Compare your responses to those of a partner for similarities and differences.

REFLECTION OF MEANING

The purpose of reflecting meaning is to explore the values and beliefs underlying the interview. Two people may experience the same event, such as an interview, but it may have a different meaning for each of them. The search for meaning is an important goal for most people, and even when the meaning is not explicitly mentioned in the interview, reflecting back on implicit meaning can be a useful skill for interviewing.

The functions of reflecting meaning are to help the interviewees interpret their feelings and actions accurately, to explore values or goals, and to understand deeper aspects of an interviewee's experience. It will not be appropriate to explore these deeper meanings in all interviews, but it will be important for the interviewer to have the skill to perceive the meanings nonetheless.

To assess your skill in reflecting meanings discuss an interaction you had with someone whose beliefs and values were different from your own, and describe those differences to your partner. Identify how these different meanings might influence an interview.

The accurate reflection of meaning in multicultural counseling means identifying a balance of apparent inconsistencies in cultural differences to achieve a balance of factors. This definition of balance is more than reconciling dissonance, as indicated by consistency theory, which seeks to avoid, change, ignore, or transcend it. The reflection of a meaningful balance to a culturally different client is better described as a tolerance for inconsistency and dissonance (Pedersen, 1990). This more complicated definition of balance means finding and reflecting meaning in both pleasure and pain, rather than merely resolving conflict to increase pleasure. The reflection and restoration of this meaningful balance is a continuous and not episodic process, reflecting the organic metaphors of holistic systems. Problems, pain, and otherwise negative aspects of our experience make an essential contribution to the ecological analysis of multicultural psychology. Chinese perspectives on yin and yang have recognized the importance of a meaningful balance for many centuries.

The reflection of meaning contributes to balance in multicultural counseling by identifying different or conflicting culturally learned perspectives without necessarily resolving them in favor of either viewpoint. Healthy and meaningful functioning in a multicultural context may require maintaining multiple conflicting but culturally learned roles without resolving the dissonance. Pedersen (1990) described ten counseling skills for reflecting meaning in a balanced perspective.

1. The ability to see positive implications in an otherwise negative experience from the client's cultural viewpoint.

2. The ability to anticipate potential negative implications from an otherwise positive experience to achieve multiple perspectives.

3. The ability to articulate statements of meaning that interpret or integrate positive and negative events in a constructive way without requiring the client to resolve resulting dissonance.

4. The ability to avoid simple solutions to complex problems and acknowledge the complicated constraints of a client's cultural context.

5. The ability to increase sensitivity about ways collective forces influence an individual's behavior.

6. The ability to increase the perceived power of the person being interviewed over time in culturally appropriate ways.

7. The ability to increase the perceived power of the person being interviewed across topics in culturally appropriate ways.

8. The ability to increase the perceived power of the person being interviewed across social roles in culturally appropriate ways.

9. The ability to adjust interviewer influence to facilitate the growth and development of culturally different clients.

10. The ability to maintain harmony within the interview in culturally appropriate ways.

The reflection of meaning becomes an important means of defining and maintaining a harmonious rapport between clients and counselors from different cultures. These examples and skills for the reflection of a meaningful balance are rooted in the traditional counseling research literature and are not, by themselves, controversial.

Frankl's 1963 work on logotherapy built a whole theory of counseling on the search for meaning and purpose in life. Logotherapy is a form of existentialism that describes meaninglessness as the primary problem of our age, causing many clients to seek counseling for that reason alone. Counseling helps clients find meaning and purpose in several ways. Frankl uses the skill of reflection to help clients discover positive meaning in even negative events. Direct reflection might, however, result in continued focusing on the negative, especially if the client dwells on the problem too much.

Ivey (1988) makes a similar point in advocating a "positive asset search" as a counseling skill. Identifying positive assets gives the interview an optimistic emphasis and helps the client increase personal power through the interview. Without denying the reality of negative aspects, the counselor might identify the thoughts, feelings, and behaviors that are positive for the client, find positive features even in a serious problem, and reframe negative self-statements. By highlighting these assets the client's development may be enhanced, identifying sources of support and promoting positive change.

Ellis (Corey, 1991) developed rational-emotive therapy to reeducate clients through persuasion and direction by removing irrational beliefs through logical argument with clients. Counseling helps clients accept their imperfect selves and prevents illogical beliefs from controlling our lives. It seeks to reflect back meaning in order to remove self-defeating beliefs and irrational thinking. The skill for doing that includes (1) identifying "A," the activating event; (2) intervening rationally to reframe "B," the beliefs about that event; and (3) changing "C," the consequences of the event, toward more rational conclusions. A skilled counselor changes consequences not by changing events but by changing the beliefs about events. Changing beliefs requires a reflection of meaning. Rational Emotive Therapy (RET) is likely to be less successful in cultures that value dependency more than self-sufficiency.

Michenbaum's cognitive behavior modification (Corey, 1991) uses self-instruction for changing the way a client thinks. Clients need to monitor their own internal dialogue and understand how they perceive themselves to understand how they are perceived by others. When these maladaptive thoughts are reflected back to the client, and the client learns new ways to cope with and solve problems, positive change occurs. Michenbaum's cognitive restructuring requires that: (1) clients observe themselves and their own behavior; (2) clients learn a new internal dialogue that is less maladaptive; and (3) learn new skills for constructive coping. Reflection of meaning helps the counselor understand the client and build a relationship, identify alternative meanings to facilitate coping, interpret culturally ambiguous messages, and assist the client in transferring new meanings to the real world.

Carl Rogers is best known for his reflection of feeling but, like other humanists and existentialists, the reflection of meaning also becomes an important way to help the client fully encounter reality. Congruent, accepting, and empathetic counselors reflect both feeling and meaning not as a technique but as an extension of themselves on a shared journey with the client toward positive growth.

Cormier and Cormier (1991) discuss cognitive modeling as a means of reflecting meaning through five steps of self-instructional training: (1) the counselor models the task while reflecting out loud about what is being done; (2) the client performs the same task, following the counselor's model and getting verbal feedback; (3) the client repeats the task while reflecting out loud about what is being done; (4) the client whispers the instructions while modeling the task; (5) the client repeats the task, monitoring the process through internal dialogue. Many other behavioral approaches for monitoring cognitive processes, like structured learning, follow a similar sequence of events in skill building.

Whenever the counselor and the client work together, there are three conversations going on at the same time. The first conversation is the explicit verbal exchange between them. The second is the counselor's internal dialogue. The third is the client's internal dialogue. The counselor can monitor the verbal exchange and his or her own internal dialogue but can only speculate on the client's internal dialogue. There are two things that can be assumed about the client's internal dialogue, however: Part of what the client is thinking will be positive and part will be negative. In order to work with culturally different clients it will be particularly important for counselors to be accurate in reflecting back the positive and negative feelings and meanings in the client's internal dialogue (Pedersen, 1988). The following exercise will provide an opportunity to practice this skill.

EXERCISE 8.3: MONITORING INTERNAL DIALOGUE

In order to focus directly on reflection of meaning skills it will be useful for you to monitor your own internal dialogue as well as the probable—your best guess—internal dialogue of your culturally different client. Write in your own and your client's internal dialogue for the following four synthetic cultures.

The Alpha Client

"I am very fortunate to be so well cared for by my family and by persons such as yourself. I try to be conscientious in obeying the rules and respecting my betters, but my family must not be pleased with what I am doing since they sent me to you. I hope you will help me so that I can make a better contribution in the future. I promise to be a good and worthy client, following any advice you give me."

Client internal dialogue:

Counselor internal dialogue:

The Beta Client

"Life certainly is full of surprises and most of them are not good. Here I sit wasting my time doing God only knows what, while I could be somewhere else. If I only knew what my family wanted, I could do it, but they don't know themselves what they want. I wonder if you have any idea yourself. I know this much: Things can't keep going on as they have been."

Client internal dialogue:

Counselor internal dialogue:

The Gamma Client

"Well, I came here, so what do you have in mind for me? I don't enjoy playing games, so just tell me what you want and let's get on with it. You should be able to teach me some new strategies so I can get along better with my family, if you're any good. We don't have to like one another to work together, you know."

Client internal dialogue:

Counselor internal dialogue:

The Delta Client

"Isn't that a crock? Me coming here to see you? I'm the one who has been successful in our family, and now they send me to see a shrink like I'm some kind of wimp. You sit there looking at me with that loosey-goosey look in your eye. What the hell do you know about anything? I'll tell you this: if you don't prove yourself this session, there's no way in hell I'm coming back!"

Client internal dialogue:

Counselor internal dialogue:

By monitoring your own internal dialogue and speculating on the client's internal dialogue, you will have a better idea of the client's meaning and cognitive process as well as his or her feelings about being in counseling. Pedersen (1988) has developed a training model that assigns counselors in training to work with three persons from the same other culture: one as a coached client, one as a coached anti-counselor, and one as a coached pro-counselor. The aim of this training model is to help counselors monitor both the negative and positive messages in a client's internal dialogue.

EMPATHY COMBINES FEELING AND MEANING

The client's response will include both affective feeling data and cognitive meaning data, and the counselor's job is to reflect back both sets of messages. Sometimes those messages are congruent, sometimes they are not. As a counselor your first task is to differentiate affect from content. The basic attending skills discussed earlier will help you in that task. As a result of understanding both affect and content the counselor is in a better position to demonstrate empathy. Empathy is experiencing the world as if you were the client. Empathy is not sympathy—what you would feel if *you* were in that situation. Egan (1986) describes empathy as "the ability to enter into and understand the world of another person and to communicate this understanding to him or her" (p. 95). Basic empathy can be viewed as a superficial communication skill, as a useful professional contract with a client, or—at the deepest level—a way of being with others. Empathy is the ability to communicate understanding—or affective/cognitive meaning—to a client. Egan describes failures at establishing empathy that can result from not responding when a response is expected, asking a question that changes focus, spouting a cliché that may seem flippant, giving an interpretation that may seem presumptuous, moving to action that may seem premature, or in some other way failing to make contact with the meaning in what the client has said.

Ivey (1988) talks about "additive empathy," which goes beyond the surface understanding of a client to add ideas or feelings that help the client further explore alternatives. Empathy can add to the client's resources just as the lack of empathy can subtract from them. Inaccurate empathy will result from inattention and inadequate use of the attending skills discussed earlier. Pretending to understand is also unlikely to result in empathy. Simplistic repeating back only and exactly what the client said will also not move the interview forward. Egan (1986) provides a list of useful suggestions for the use of basic empathy.

1. Empathy is a way of being and not just a professional role or skill.
2. Attend to the physical and psychological viewpoint.
3. Set aside your own biases and judgments.
4. Listen for the core message in what the client says.
5. Listen for both verbal and nonverbal messages.
6. Respond fairly frequently but briefly.
7. Be flexible and tentative to give the client room.
8. Be gentle, and keep focused on primary issues.
9. Respond to experiences, behaviors, and feelings alike.
10. Move toward exploring sensitive topics.
11. Check if your empathic response was on target.
12. Determine if your empathic response is helpful.
13. Note signs of stress and the reason for being stressed.
14. Keep focused on helping the client.

Goldstein and Michaels (1985) describe the affective-cognitive-communication features of empathy as described by Keefe (1976) as the most comprehensive description of empathy. In Keefe's description the first phase of empathy is the perception of a feeling stage and thoughts in another person by means of the other person's behaviors. The second phase is generating a feeling and cognitive response not as stereotyping, judging, or classifying but more like experiencing the other person's world. The third stage involves detachment and decoding the feelings and thoughts through labeling, sorting out, and separating the counselor's from the client's perspective. Finally, the counselor communicates accurate feedback to the other person to demonstrate the condition of empathy. Empathy is neither sympathy nor projection, wherein a counselor might confuse a client's feeling with what he or she would feel under similar conditions. Empathy is not identification, an attempt to be like the client.

TRAINING COUNSELORS TO INCREASE THEIR EMPATHY

Goldstein and Michaels (1985) describe six major training approaches for developing empathy. The first is a didactic-experiential design based on work by Truax and Carkhuff. This approach involves extensive readings, followed by listening to and watching taped materials where empathy is displayed, followed by role-playing and finally participation in interviews with clients. This process is designed to lead participants through five levels of empathic understanding.

A second training approach is Gerard Egan's "interpersonal living laboratory." This approach involves a variety of human-relations training skills with participants receiving didactic instruction within a group context where those skills can be used. The participant develops from primary level accurate empathy to advanced accurate empathy where the implicit implications as well as the explicit feelings and thoughts of the other person are understood and articulated.

A third training approach involves "relationship enhancement" based on work by Bernard Guerney, emphasizing skills in using expressive and empathic responses, relationship enhancement, plus facilitator abilities to teach these skills to others. The skills are taught using social learning techniques that include (1) rapport building; (2) detailed explanation, presentation, discussion, and elaboration; (3) modeling the skills; (4) practicing the skills with feedback; and (5) applying the skills.

A fourth training approach involves microtraining to enrich intimacy, based on work by Allen Ivey. It involves (1) teaching behaviors that go along with respect; (2) teaching behaviors that go along with empathy; (3) teaching behaviors of genuineness; (4) integrating these components through role-playing practice sessions with feedback; and (5) generalizing the skill to real-world situations.

A fifth training approach involves structured learning as developed by Arnold Goldstein and others. It begins by modeling empathy either through live demonstrations or the media. This is followed by trainees role-playing the skills of empathy as they saw those skills demonstrated in the models. The third step is getting feedback on how well they demonstrated empathy. The final step is transferring what they learned in the training session to the real world.

The sixth training approach uses programmed self-instruction. The trainee goes through a series of programmed exercises to move the trainee's skill level through increased awareness of interpersonal perceptual processes by both correcting errors and identifying the antecedents or consequences of empathy in a gestalt mode.

There are many other training methods being used to teach empathy. The diversity of approaches reflects the diversity of ways that empathy is defined as a construct. Goldstein and Michaels (1985) advocate teaching the components of empathy in an eclectic design that begins with readiness training in preparatory skills such as imagination, observation, flexibility, and differentiation. The second stage involves training in perception so that the person perceives accurately and with sensitivity. The third stage relates to affective reverberation training such as mediation, structural integration, bioenergetics, focusing, or some other sensory awareness training. The fourth stage involves cognitive analysis training involving nonevaluative and objective recording of the other person's behavior where the observer steps back and accurately labels the other person's affective-cognitive perspective. The fifth stage is communication training using several of the many different social learning approaches designed to enhance communication skills. The sixth stage is to transfer and maintain the skill level reached through training. This is the weakest link in the training sequence when skills have either not been transferred to the real world or have not been maintained over time.

Empathy is elusive in combining both the reflection of feelings and the reflection of meaning skills. However, research on counseling in multicultural settings suggests that establishing an empathic relationship is the single most important necessary but not sufficient factor to identify successful counseling.

KEY IDEAS

1. The purpose of reflecting of feeling skills.
   Provide feedback on feelings that are being displayed.
   Clarify the role of feelings in the interview.
   Identify and expand the pool of feeling words being used.
2. Reflection of feeling skills.
   Identify and clarify mixed feelings in the interviewee.
   Help the interviewee face up to feelings.
   Check out inferences about what the interviewee might be feeling.
   Hold reflection of feeling feedback until the right time.
   Explore metaphors the interviewee uses to express feelings.

3. The purpose of reflection of meaning skills.
    To explore the values and beliefs underlying the interview.
    To help interpret feelings and actions accurately.

4. Reflection of meaning skills.
    Interpret the meaning of feelings displayed by the interviewee.
    Explore alternative interpretations of what is being said.
    Establish a priority of interpretations or explanations.
    Check out whether the reflection of meaning was accurate.
    Frankl's logotherapy emphasizes the search for meaning.
    Ivey's positive asset search identifies positive meaning.
    Ellis seeks to reduce irrational beliefs.
    Michenbaum emphasizes cognitive restructuring.
    Rogers finds meaning in the shared journey.
    Cormier and Cormier discuss cognitive modeling.
    Pedersen seeks to explicate a client's internal dialogue.

5. Empathy combines feeling and meaning.
    Feelings and meaning are essential to demonstrating empathy.
    Egan describes basic and advanced empathy.
    Ivey describes additive empathy.
    Goldstein and Michaels discuss phases of empathy.

6. Training counselors to increase their empathy.
    Truax and Carkhuff present a didactic-experiential method.
    Egan discusses an interpersonal living laboratory method.
    Guerney teaches relationship enhancement.
    Ivey suggests microtraining methods to develop empathy.
    Goldstein describes empathy modeling as a method.
    Goldstein and Michaels teach the components of empathy.

EXERCISE 8.4: REFLECTION OF FEELING AND MEANING SKILLS

The following role-play will provide an opportunity for you to practice doing reflection of feeling and reflection of meaning in an interview setting.

1. Form a three-person group with one of you being the interviewer from one synthetic culture, one the interviewee from a different synthetic culture, and one the observer.

2. Select an interview situation and conduct a ten-minute role-played interview, followed by a ten-minute discussion by the observer on how the reflection of feeling and meaning were done.

3. Exchange roles so that all three persons have an opportunity to be interviewer, interviewee, and observer.

Instructions for the observer: Listen for examples of reflection of feeling and reflection of meaning skills as they are used in the interview. Pay particular attention to (1) how reflection was shaped by the counselor's own cultural perspective, and (2) how reflection might or might not be appropriate to the client's cultural perspective.

1. Identify and clarify mixed feelings in the interview.
   Example:

2. Help the interviewee face up to feelings.
   Example:

3. Check out inferences about what the interviewee might be feeling.
   Example:

4. Hold reflection of feeling feedback until the right time.
   Example:

5. Explore metaphors the interviewee uses to express feelings.
   Example:

6. Interpret the meaning of feelings displayed by the interviewee.
   Example:

7. Explore alternative interpretations of what is being said.
   Example:

8. Explore a priority of interpretations or explanations.
   Example:

9. Check out whether the reflection of meaning was accurate.
   Example:

Chapter Nine

Confrontation and Mediation Skills

Major Objective:
To understand the meaning of conflict and confrontation with culturally different clients.

Secondary Objectives:
1. To identify alternative means for confronting culturally different clients.
2. To anticipate the alternative responses to confrontation by culturally different clients.
3. To demonstrate the characteristics of mediating multicultural conflict.

Confrontation and mediation are some of the most difficult culture-centered counseling skills. Confronting discrepancies in the interview is important to clarify confusion and to verify the accuracy of information collected. Persons with good confrontation and mediation skills will be able to point out incongruities, discrepancies, and mixed messages in a person's behavior, thoughts, feelings, or meanings, using the skills covered in earlier chapters of this book. These skills will give clients an opportunity to explain and resolve or better manage cultural differences within themselves or between themselves and others.

IDENTIFYING AND MANAGING CONFLICT

Conflict is a natural part of any situation where more than one person is involved. The conflict may be positive (functional) or negative (dysfunctional). When it is negative, conflict threatens to erode the consensus that brings a group together. When it is positive, the conflict is usually about less central issues and takes place within the context of a general consensus. Positive conflict can actually strengthen group relationships, especially if different members of the conflicting groups share common ground.

As long as there is a basic consensus across groups, there may be many conflicts among them. The smaller conflicts might actually strengthen them by preventing two groups from polarizing on a particular central issue. A simple polarized split on one central issue is less complicated but much more likely to destroy one or both groups. It is important to distinguish between interpersonal conflict and organizational conflict.

Interpersonal conflict is usually caused by different perceptions, or how persons view an event, a person, or an idea. Each person has learned to perceive facts differently: (1) Ideological differences are learned as belief systems that are usually beyond discussion and do not require proof to be believed. (2) Personality differences have resulted from culturally learned styles of preferred behavior. (3) Status differences have resulted from a culture or society's level of recognition granted to the individual.

Organizational conflicts are more likely to happen when changes of function, role, or process are introduced to a group or groups. (1) Unclear delegation of authority or responsibility will cause conflict. (2) Inadequate supervision will cause conflict. (3) Incomplete delegation will cause conflict, especially when a person has responsibility without corresponding authority. (4) Unclear goals or methods for achieving goals will cause conflict when members of a group have different criteria for success.

In responding to conflict there are several choices. Doing nothing or avoiding direct conflict is one alternative. The decision not to get involved is more than inaction. Referring the matter to a subordinate is also different from doing nothing. Delegation of authority requires skill and experience. Assuming that conflicts are best solved closest to their origin, delegating conflict-resolving authority might be a good choice, as long as the authority is clearly delegated.

Taking a hard line that is closed and authoritarian is a second alternative. Such an approach might refer to organizational charts and policy precedents or some other basis of nonarbitrary authority. For interpersonal conflicts the hard line might stress the importance of controlling personal feelings for the good of the group. In any case this alternative requires a leader's strong presence.

A third alternative is to take a soft line that is supportive and open. Here the solution to conflict might be shaped around the people involved, delegating authority to some and urging others to respect that authority. For interpersonal conflicts you could allow persons to ventilate feelings and then participate in developing solutions.

No single strategy will work best in all situations of conflict resolution, especially when that conflict is multicultural. In each case a combination of strategies would probably be preferred. It is important to draw from all available alternatives, determining opportunities for flexibility as well as the necessity for firmness. It is also important to develop back-up strategies when things don't happen as you expected (Astin, 1978).

Sometimes the interviewer's task will be to work through the discrepancies with the client, as when an employee comes in late, has failed in an assigned responsibility, or has created some sort of problem in the organization. If confrontation is handled poorly, the interview will result in one or both persons becoming angry or embarrassed, and then the problem is much larger. The feedback skills discussed earlier provide some guidelines for how confrontation can be handled effectively. If confrontation is handled poorly, one or both persons will lose.

CONFRONTATION SKILLS

If confrontation is handled skillfully, then the interview and the relationship can continue without either person becoming angry or embarrassed. Since different persons and cultures have different rules for handling confrontation, it is useful to begin by discussing the rules for confrontation. The more specific and less general the confrontation, the more likely it is to confront successfully. If confrontation is handled skillfully, it is possible for both persons or groups to win.

In order to check out your level of confrontation skill, work with a partner and identify how you would confront a client in the three following situations. Compare your responses with your partner's. Discuss why each of you gave a particular response. In each case presume that the client was from a cultural background very different from your own.

1. A client was late in arriving for counseling every day for a long period of time.
2. A counselor whom you supervise has hired a relative or friend whom you do not believe to be competent for the job.
3. Your supervisor has failed to promote you, even though you have done better work than your colleagues.

It is more difficult to confront someone who is higher than yourself in authority and power than someone who is below you in the organizational structure. However, the same skills apply in either case, and the consequences of skillful confrontation or mediation are potentially as valuable.

Confrontation and mediation skills build on and incorporate all the skills reviewed in previous chapters. These skills will help counselors (1) identify the discrepancy and (2) incorporate the discrepancy into the counseling process. The first task is to locate the discrepancy.

First of all, the discrepancy might be within the client's own mixed messages and incongruities, which come through as a confused or argumentative internal dialogue.

Second, the discrepancy might be between two client statements.

Third, the discrepancy might be between what the client says and does, reminding one of the saying, "Watch what they do and not what they say."

Fourth, the discrepancy might be between verbal and nonverbal messages.

Fifth, the discrepancy might be between two nonverbal messages.

Sixth, the discrepancy might be between what the client says and the problem or real-world context.

Seventh, the discrepancy might be between two or more persons.

Eighth, the discrepancy might be seen as a cross-cultural conflict.

The second task is to incorporate the discrepancy into the counseling processes. Ivey (1988) points out that sometimes labeling the discrepancy is enough to solve the situation. When that is not enough, however, it is useful to use the rules for giving feedback, listening and attending, questioning, paraphrasing, and summarizing to help the client confront the conflict. In some cases it is not possible or perhaps not necessary to resolve the conflict but rather only necessary to help the client manage the discrepancy more effectively on a more permanent basis. Ivey suggests that clients functioning at lower developmental levels experience more discrepancy and conflict than those working at higher developmental levels. Cultures deal with conflict in a variety of ways, as we will see with the synthetic cultures, and sometimes conflict may indicate a higher level of positive functioning.

In general terms the counselor will probably deal with conflict in one of the three ways mentioned earlier. The first approach is to do nothing, the second is to take a hard line, and the third is to take a soft line. To do nothing may indicate a conscious or unconscious preference to ignore the conflict rather than deal with it, but it is a conscious decision not to get involved. The counselor may refer the matter to someone else rather than deal with it, moving the conflict farther from its source of origin and giving subordinates the impression of cowardice. To take a hard line is to take a closed and authoritarian perspective. Conflicts in organizations are solved administratively, while interpersonal conflict would be solved in whatever way was advantageous to the organization. To take a soft line is to be more open and supportive. Organizational conflict would be dealt with by delegating more authority and encouraging others to respect authority. Interpersonal conflict would be dealt with by eliciting individual feelings from the conflicting persons to ventilate their feelings and participate in the solution. There is a variety of different overlapping but distinct and specific strategies for confronting conflict.

MODELS FOR CONFRONTING CONFLICT

It is important to review the several most prominent approaches in the literature for confronting conflict in counseling. Goldstein and Rosenbaum

(1982) discuss several ways to deal with aggression or conflict in yourself or in others.

The first way is through meditation or learning to focus on your bodily sensations/feelings as a way of blocking out the outside-world conflict.

A second way is to monitor your own internal dialogue and teach yourself new ways to handle the conflict, just as you might teach someone else. Your angry response to conflict becomes a signal to look more closely at yourself and monitor your own internal dialogue to encourage the positive messages and discourage the negative.

A third strategy is to calm the others involved in the conflict, focusing on defeating the problem rather than the other person. The counseling skills in earlier chapters provide tools to calm others, such as listening, understanding, reassuring, and attending.

A fourth strategy is to focus on the communication process as potentially problem-solving rather than conflict-producing. To do this you might use the feedback skills discussed earlier and build empathy with the other person.

A fifth strategy is to negotiate win-win outcomes for those in conflict. If win-win solutions are not available, you might resort to compromises, as long as you avoid the lose-lose or a polarized win-lose outcome that would likely prolong the negative conflict.

The sixth strategy is contracting, with both persons working out their responsibilities toward the other and their expected rewards.

Goldstein and Rosenbaum (1982) go on to describe a "structured learning" skill-building sequence of behavioral steps for dealing with conflict through discussion, modeling, rehearsing, and transferring the skill to real conflict.

Cormier and Cormier (1991) describe confrontation as one means of helping clients explore alternative ways of perceiving themselves or the situation that can lead to new choices. Confrontation will also help clients become aware of discrepancies or incongruities in what they do, feel, or think. A good confrontation will not make the client defensive. They suggest ground rules to help that happen.

1. Be aware of your own motives for confronting the client at this time and place about this topic. Don't use confrontation to attack the client or get rid of your own frustration.

2. Before you confront be sure you have established rapport and trust with the client. Don't confront unless you are willing to stick around and help the client pick up the pieces.

3. Wait until the right time to confront, when the client is ready to use this information constructively. Hit-and-run confrontation is not helpful.

4. Don't overload the client with confronting messages. You might become more painful than the original problem if you come on too strong.

5. Recognize the limits of confrontation that can bring about limited awareness insight. Not all insight results in change.

However good you are in using confrontation skills, the outcome will be successful or unsuccessful depending on the client's response to your confrontation.

Confrontation and mediation skills are those ways in which an interviewer reflects back implicit or explicit disagreements from the interview. Ivey (1988) points out that conflict can be constructive, depending on how the client responds. Ivey presents five levels for measuring a client's response to conflict, from a lower to a higher level.

1. The lowest level response would be to deny that there is any disagreement or mixed message at all.

2. A slightly higher level response would be a partial examination or willingness to admit to some disagreement.

3. A third higher level response would be a willingness to examine the situation completely and admit to the disagreement, even while being unwilling to change anything.

4. A fourth higher level response would be the recognition of a disagreement, but with the client choosing to compromise or accommodate the problem.

5. The fifth and highest level response would be where the client develops new ways to change that will either eliminate the disagreement or incorporate the dissonance into a higher quality level of functioning.

Egan (1990) discusses ways that the client might deny a confrontation, including: first, discrediting the counselor; second, persuading the counselor that his or her views are wrong; third, devaluing the importance of the topic; fourth, seeking support elsewhere; and fifth, agreeing with the confrontation but not doing anything about it. Egan (1985) presents a strategy for confronting conflict in which one dimension focuses on degrees of assertiveness (concern with your own needs and wants or the needs and wants of your organization) and degrees of responsiveness (sensitivity to the needs and wants of others). A high degree of assertiveness plus a low degree of responsiveness will result in a preference to compete, command, fight, order, or demand. On the other hand, a style that combines a low degree of assertiveness with a high degree of responsiveness might give in when confronted. Each person has a preferred style, and each style has both advantages and disadvantages. Egan's strategy includes five different styles of conflict-managing behaviors.

1. Commanding combines a high assertiveness with low responsiveness.

2. Avoiding combines low assertiveness with low responsiveness.

3. Giving in or accommodating combines low assertiveness with high responsiveness.

4. Compromising combines moderate assertiveness with moderate responsiveness.

5. Collaborating combines high assertiveness with high responsiveness.

Goldstein and Segall (1983) offer a strategy for confronting conflict that looks at the way diverse variables interact to influence aggressive behavior, linking ecocultural forces, socialization practice, individual experiences, and individual behavioral dispositions whenever frustrations need to be overcome and conflicts need to be resolved. According to this model of aggression the conflict begins in an ecocultural context through individual experiences; second, moves to the interpersonal situation involving competition or frustration; third, moves to psychological constructs including the person's personal disposition as well as provocative situations; and fourth, moves to the observed behaviors of conflict and aggression. Confrontation skills are useful when they interrupt or mediate to prevent that chain of events that moves toward aggressive acts.

EXERCISE 9.1: SELECTING A STRATEGY FOR CONFRONTING CONFLICT

Identify three alternatives for dealing with a particular incident of multicultural conflict.

First, identify a "hard" alternative where radical change and direct or strong confrontation would be required. In this alternative the conflict will not be avoided or minimized but actually sought out so that there is a clear winner and a clear loser.

Second, identify a "soft" alternative where compromise and appeasement is encouraged. In this alternative you will seek to avoid or minimize the conflict so that each side will win some advantages but lose others.

Third, identify the strategy of "denial" where all parties continue on their separate ways, neither confronting nor avoiding conflict.

Work together in a group of five or six participants. Identify a situation involving multicultural conflict affecting a clearly identified client from the newspaper or some other source known to all members of the group. Working independently, respond to the following five tasks:

1. Work out a list of all the strategies you can think of for the client to confront conflict productively in this situation. After writing down each strategy indicate whether it is hard, soft, or moderate.

2. Choose one or a combination of your alternatives that you think would work best for the client, and describe why.

3. To what extent is your best-choice strategy flexible, offering the client room to modify your confrontation?

4. To what extent is your best-choice strategy firm and uncompromising?
5. What is your back-up plan if your strategy for the client doesn't go as you expect/predict?

When all members have independently completed answering the above five questions, respond as a group to the following tasks:

1. Draw up one main strategy for dealing with the multicultural conflict situation.
2. Choose one or two back-up plans in case things don't work out as expected.
3. Evaluate the approaches suggested by individuals in your group for solving the situation according to Ivey's five levels of client response (1988). Score the alternative responses.

To the extent that there was real disagreement and the alternative tended to deny it, give that alternative 1 point.

To the extent that the alternative recommended a partial examination or willingness to recognize real disagreements, even though no action was taken, give that alternative 2 points.

To the extent that the alternative recommended a full examination or willingness to recognize real disagreements, even though no action was taken, give that alternative 3 points.

To the extent that the alternative recommended a full examination or willingness to recognize real disagreements, even though the clients deliberately chose to accommodate or compromise, give that alternative 4 points.

To the extent that the alternative recommended a full examination or willingness to recognize real disagreements and new creative ways were identified to change the situation in positive ways, give that alternative 5 points.

Add up the scores for the different alternatives, and discuss the differences between high-scoring and low-scoring alternatives.

MEDIATION SKILLS

In addition to looking at confrontation skills it is useful to consider the slightly different but similar range of mediation skills in the multicultural situation. Goldstein (1986) defines an intercultural mediation as any mediation situation where two or more of the participants identify themselves with different cultural groups. She includes both situations where those cultural differences are among the disputants and/or between disputants and mediators. Goldstein suggests that a successful approach will need to combine both culture-specific and culture-general perspectives. Multicultural mediation requires a relationship that includes attention to both the similarities across cultures and differences between cultures. Overemphasis on either similarities or differences will result in failure.

Mediation is defined as the actions of a neutral third party who, at the request of conflicting parties, assists in establishing an acceptable resolution of their conflicts. Mediation differs from arbitration, because arbitration imposes a settlement on both parties and differs from litigation in that litigants each attempt to win in a formal meeting. Mediation focuses the responsibility for conflict resolution on the people most directly involved. The stages of mediation include ventilation, information gathering, problem solving, and bargaining, usually in that order.

Culture is often used ambiguously with regard to mediation in the literature. Janosik (1987) describes four distinct approaches to culture in the negotiation/mediation literature.

The first approach describes culture as simply learned behavior, providing a cookbook approach that is overly simplistic in its analysis.

The second approach describes culture as a shared value which, while admitting to slightly more complex variation, relies on stereotypes to describe relationships among groups.

The third approach describes culture as dialectic in a way that acknowledges within-group differences but relies on probabilistic prediction to identify general but dynamic tendencies within each group.

The fourth approach describes culture in a context and provides both the most complicated and most accurate approach to understanding it. The individual's personality, cultural values, and social context combine to influence behavior.

This multi-casual approach is favored by academic analysts but is usually considered too inconvenient for practitioners. In all cases culture is acknowledged as important, but the problem is how to identify the link between culture and behavior in such a way that mediation can be both accurate and convenient.

Sunoo (1990) suggests that one possible means of clarifying the link between culture and conflicting behaviors is in the separation of behaviors from expectations, emphasizing how two parties experiencing conflict might be similar and different at the same time without knowing it. In Chapter Two we discussed the Cultural Grid as a tool to identify and describe the cultural aspects of situations and train people for culturally appropriate interaction in multicultural settings. We discussed the Intrapersonal Cultural Grid, which looks at the locus of culture inside the person and the network of social-system variables that have taught us the values that shape our expectations and determine our behaviors. We also discussed the Interpersonal Cultural Grid, which shows the importance of identifying aspects of the conflict where the two persons or groups share the same expectations but express them through different, incongruent behaviors. If a counselor can identify the common ground of shared expectations, then conflicting behaviors can be tolerated or perhaps even mobilized as a creative resource across a shared expectation of friendship.

In mediating multicultural conflict it is important not to be distracted by very different and dissonant behaviors without first seeking out the positive expectations and values behind them. It is also important to identify the culturally learned common ground of culturally similar positive expectations and values that can then become a foundation for the mediation process (Duryea, 1992).

Review Chapter Two on the Cultural Grid, and then practice using that strategy to mediate conflict between two synthetic cultures. In mediating multicultural conflict the following four steps provide a framework for facilitation.

1. Identify one or more specific behaviors of an individual or conflicting behaviors among several individuals from culturally different backgrounds.

2. Identify the positive expectations each person or persons attaches to the behavior. What is expected to happen as a result of that behavior? There will probably be several positive expectations attached to each.

3. Identify the values each person or persons attaches to culturally learned positive expectations. What are the underlying values in which that expectation is grounded that make it important and meaningful?

4. Identify the social-system variables where those values have been taught to the person or persons so that you can understand the basis for the cultural values that led to the expectations that led to the behavior.

EXERCISE 9.2: MEDIATING MULTICULTURAL CONFLICT

Examine examples of conflict between the following synthetic cultures and identify examples of common ground in positive expectations and/or values that persons from both share. Refer to the guidelines on synthetic cultures in Chapter Three to help you identify these.

Conflict between an Alpha and a Beta

Alphas emphasize a hierarchy of power where each person has her or his place, showing respect to those above and expecting obedience from those below. Betas dislike uncertainty and do not tolerate ambiguity, so there is a structure of laws that must be obeyed and goes beyond the needs of individuals or society. A possible conflict between Alpha and Beta might be a high power-level group of Alphas who do whatever they like and disregard the rules, in spite of objection by Betas in that society.

Conflict between an Alpha and a Gamma

Alphas emphasize a hierarchy of power where each person has her or his place, showing respect to those above and expecting obedience from those below. Gammas are individualistic and believe everyone should take care of themselves and remain emotionally independent of groups, organizations, or society. A possible conflict between Alphas and Gammas might be a group of Gammas who fail to show proper respect for Alpha leaders.

Conflict between an Alpha and a Delta

Alphas emphasize a hierarchy of power where each person has her or his place, showing respect to those above and expecting obedience from those below. Deltas are assertive, materialistic, and success oriented, seeking rapid progress and ultimate domination in their relationships with others. A possible conflict would be a group of Deltas who attack the Alpha hierarchy as uneconomic and inefficient and attempt to remove the Alphas from power.

Conflict between a Beta and a Gamma

Betas avoid uncertainty whenever possible and prefer a structure of clear, unambiguous rules to define truth and duty in their relationships. Gammas are individualistic and believe everyone should take care of themselves and remain emotionally independent of groups, organizations, society. A possible conflict between Betas and Gammas might be the increased power by Gammas who promote individual freedom where everyone can do whatever they want and where nobody has a right to control their behavior.

Conflict between a Beta and a Delta

Betas avoid uncertainty whenever possible and prefer a structure of clear, unambiguous rules to define truth and duty in their relationships. Deltas are assertive, materialistic, and success oriented, seeking rapid progress and ultimate domination in their relationships with others. A possible conflict between Betas and Deltas might be the increased power by a small clique of Deltas who interpret the rules to their own advantage or find ways around the rules to increase their own power in society.

Conflict between a Gamma and a Delta

Gammas are individualistic and believe everyone should take care of themselves and remain emotionally independent from groups, organizations, or society. Deltas are assertive, materialistic, and success oriented, seeking rapid progress and ultimate domination in their relationships with others. A possible conflict between Gammas and Deltas might be a power struggle where the Deltas use teamwork in their organization to destroy individualistic Gammas and take over society.

FINDING COMMON GROUND

The most difficult part of mediating multicultural conflict is finding common ground. Mediators should begin by seeking "favorable conditions" for contact between conflicting parties. These favorable conditions require that neither side lose status, that both sides seek cooperation, that authority figures support the mediation, and that bargaining parties have the flexibility to change. These conditions do not happen spontaneously but are the products of hard work by skilled mediators (Amir, 1969; Miller and Brewer, 1984).

The success of multicultural mediation depends on finding common ground or shared expectations between the two conflicting parties. Rubin, Kim, and Peretz (1990) discuss the difficulties in accurately identifying another person's expectations: (1) Multicultural conflict may be based on misattributions, but both parties will respond to their perception of reality, whether true or not. (2) There is usually a lack of reliable or complete information about what others expect, resulting in partisan expectations by both parties. (3) Both culturally different parties typically have stereotyped expectations about one another, rather than accurate data. (4) Any perceived inaccuracy or inappropriateness in multicultural mediation will destroy the process. (5) Selective perception, attributional distortion, and self-fulfilling prophecies in mediation might increase, rather than decrease, conflict. The multicultural mediator needs to be highly skilled to avoid these problems.

The Cultural Grid, discussed earlier, already demonstrated the importance and process of separating expectations from behaviors. This process can result in joint problem solving and win-win outcomes through identifying jointly held expectations such as trust, fairness, safety, and effectiveness. In addition to promoting joint problem solving through shared expectations, it is also important not to be distracted by dissimilar and apparently hostile or contentious behavior by either or both parties. In multicultural conflict it is quite possible that the behavior is being misperceived, and misattributions would destroy the possibility of joint problem solving.

Multicultural conflict is too often described exclusively in terms of the culturally learned but different (and apparently hostile or contentious) behaviors of the parties in conflict. When two culturally different parties misattribute each other's behavior, this misattribution is likely to result in a negative chain reaction of escalating hostility.

1. The different (apparently hostile and contentious) behaviors will suggest that expectations are also different.

2. As different (apparently hostile and contentious) behaviors persist, the two persons will develop negative expectations for the future.

3. One of the two persons may be forced to modify behaviors to match the other person, but their expectations will become more divergent, hostile, and contentious.

4. Eventually the conflict is likely to become more overt, as each party attributes negative expectations to the other.

5. The conflicting parties will separate without being aware of their misattribution.

When, on the other hand, the common ground of shared expectations is discovered, the joint problem-solving process is likely to result in the following positive chain reaction.

1. The different (apparently hostile and contentious) behaviors will be understood as expressions of a shared positive expectation.

2. Both parties will identify and emphasize their shared positive expectations in a joint problem-solving format and not be distracted by their different behaviors.

3. One or both parties may voluntarily modify their behaviors to match the other person, or the two persons may agree to disagree about the appropriate behavior.

4. The common ground defined by shared positive expectations will provide a basis for joint problem solving and harmony in future relationships.

5. Both parties will become more accurate in interpreting each other's behaviors within that cultural context.

The process of finding common ground can be summarized in five steps of counselor or mediator activity:

First, identify the specific dissimilar (apparently hostile and contentious) behaviors of culturally different persons in conflict.

Second, try to identify the positive expectations, such as trust, fairness, respect, and harmony each person attaches to behavior and encourage each to interpret the other party's behavior in terms of those positive expectations accurately.

Third, try to identify the values behind each person's different behaviors and similar positive expectations, with particular attention to values that the two parties share.

Fourth, try to identify the appropriate social systems where those values were learned or taught, with particular attention to salient social systems that the two parties share.

Fifth, develop joint problem-solving strategies based on positive shared expectations, without being distracted by different (apparently hostile and contentious) behaviors of each party toward the other.

The Cultural Grid helps mediators identify the common ground of shared positive expectations so that they can accurately interpret the other person's different behaviors and prevent misattribution. The more explicit these shared positive expectations can be made, the more likely that the disputing parties will recognize their common ground for successful joint problem solving. Mediating multicultural conflict requires the accurate identification of specific behaviors in the context of expectations, values, and social systems where those behaviors were learned.

KEY IDEAS

1. The purpose of confrontation skills.
    Clarify confusion.
    Verify the accuracy of information.
    Identify incongruities, discrepancies, and mixed messages.
2. Levels of response to confrontation.
    Lowest level would deny disagreement.
    Higher level would be partial examination.
    Higher level would be to recognize disagreement but not change.
    Higher level would be to live with the disagreement.
    Highest level would be to eliminate or reduce disagreement.
3. Confrontation skills.
    Follow the rules of good feedback covered earlier.
    Be specific rather than general.
    Be explicit rather than implicit.
    Reduce your own anxiety about confrontation.
    Maintain harmony while confronting.
    Establish the rules of confrontation beforehand.
4. Models for confronting conflict.
    Goldstein and Rosenbaum's approach to conflict is to focus on internal states and solving the problem, rather than attacking for win-win outcomes.
    Goldstein and Rosenbaum apply structured learning to identify behavioral steps in conflict resolution.
    Cormier and Cormier describe five rules for "good confrontation" as a way to explore and identify new choices.

Ivey suggests five levels of client response to conflict from a lower to a higher level.

Egan focuses on degrees of assertiveness and responsiveness in five styles of conflict management.

Goldstein and Segall describe conflict in an ecocultural context in four stages of development.

5. Mediation skills.

Goldstein combines the culture-specific and culture-general perspectives in mediation.

Mediation proceeds through stages of ventilation, information gathering, problem solving, and bargaining.

Janosik describes four approaches to multicultural mediation from the least to the most complex and contextual.

Sunoo suggests the separation of behaviors from expectations as essential for multicultural mediation.

The Cultural Grid provides a structure for separating behaviors from expectations.

6. Finding common ground.

Mediation requires favorable conditions in order to work.

Joint problem solving requires identifying expectations in spite of difficulties of misattribution, misperception, and stereotypes.

The Cultural Grid provides a structure for separating positive, shared expectations from dissimilar behaviors.

The misattribution of dissimilar behaviors will result in a negative chain reaction of escalating hostility.

The accurate identification of shared positive expectations will provide common ground for joint problem solving.

Five steps for finding common ground are presented.

EXERCISE 9.3: EXERCISES IN CONFRONTATION AND MEDIATION SKILLS

In order to practice your confrontation and mediation skills you will be asked to role-play a synthetic culture in a conflict situation. By this point in your training you should have established enough trust and rapport to allow the role-playing of confrontation. Do what you can to make this a safe situation so that all participants will feel they can practice confrontation skills without offending one another.

1. Select two partners to form a three-person group, with an interviewer from one synthetic culture, an interviewee from another synthetic culture, and an observer to role-play for a ten-minute interview.

2. After the interview the observer will lead a discussion on specific examples of confrontation by the interviewer and their consequences. Attempt to grade the interviewer's response to confrontation according to the six-level Ivey scale of possible responses and/or one of the other strategies presented in this chapter.

3. Exchange roles so that each person has an opportunity to play the interviewer, interviewee, and observer.

Instructions to the observer: Listen and watch for specific examples of confrontation and mediation skills as they are used in the interview. Record verbatim statements if possible, but in any case be as specific and detailed as you can.

1. The rules for good feedback were followed.
   Example:

2. The confrontation was explicit, rather than implicit.
   Example:

3. The confronter was not anxious about confrontation.
   Example:

4. Harmony was maintained, even during confrontation.
   Example:

5. The interviewee was prepared for being confronted by the interviewer.
   Example:

6. The mediator was not distracted by different behaviors in the conflict.
   Example:

7. The mediator was able to identify common ground of shared expectations in the conflict.
   Example:

8. The mediator was able to create the favorable conditions for contact to result in more harmony.
   Example:

9. The mediator had a well-developed strategy for mediation.
   Example:

Chapter Ten

Focusing, Directing, and Interpreting Skills

Major Objective:
To synthesize and focus culture-centered counseling skills toward intentional and directed change by culturally different clients.

Secondary Objectives:

1. To identify the variety of targets for focusing with culturally different clients.

2. To demonstrate directive skills for implementing change with culturally different clients.

3. To identify the importance of accurate and intentional interpretation with culturally different clients.

By now you have reviewed the basic interviewing skills and have had an opportunity to practice them with one another, centering on your real-world cultures as well as on the four synthetic cultures. The next step is the ability to focus and direct those skills. Culture-centered counseling skills are focused on the common-ground similarity between your real world and synthetic or assumed cultures. Often the differences are most evident in people's behaviors toward one another, and the similarities are most evident in people's expectations, even though the same expectations are frequently associated with different behaviors in different cultures.

Culture-centered counseling skills are also focused on the basic underlying, culturally learned assumptions that control a person's life, where behaviors are rooted in culturally learned expectations and values. By centering on a person's culture it becomes possible to assess behaviors accurately and to understand the social-system sources of culturally learned values and expectations.

FOCUSING SKILLS: TARGETS

In order to apply the skills described in previous chapters it is important for you to focus and direct them appropriately and accurately. Think of yourself as having been given power, of having control, of being in charge of the situation. Through appropriate and accurate focusing and directing you will be able to move the interview from one place to another, at a faster or slower pace with a broader or narrower focus. You should now be able to match your perspective with your client's cultural perspective accurately. In this way you will be able to facilitate counseling outcomes that will build on the client's culturally learned values and expectations, which are already firmly in place, and increase the likelihood of gains through counseling that will transfer permanently to the real world.

Culture is both complex and dynamic. Focusing and directing skills are the ways in which an interviewer learns to increase or decrease control in the interview so that it will be more successful. Focusing will help you and your clients see the problem or situation from several alternative viewpoints. You will be able to guide the interview toward goals the client already accepts as important. You will be able to change that focus and direction as the client's cultural interpretation changes from time to time and place to place. You are a camera taking a series of photographs, with each photograph focusing on a different aspect of the mindscape. You are a flashlight in a dark room, directing light to the different parts to find your way around and to help yourself and your client explore the room's contents. You are transferring this ability to focus and direct to your clients so that they can manage their own problems in their own ways.

There are several targets on which the interviewer may want to focus.

First, the interviewee may be the focus of attention. This might mean giving attention to the client's thoughts, behaviors, feelings, or some especially important aspect of the interviewee.

Second, the focus might be on a main topic, theme, or problem. The content of the interview may sometimes, but not always, be the most important focus.

Third, the interviewer might be the target of focus. This would be particularly true if the interviewer is having a noticeable positive or negative effect on the client.

Fourth, other people might become the target of focus. There is a cultural context of relationships and support systems on which the interviewee depends which will be important to the interview.

Fifth, the family might become the target of focus. The family may symbolize a meaningful context for the client in important positive or negative ways that will facilitate the interview.

Sixth, the relationship between the interviewer and the interviewee might become the target. This relationship would be especially important when it is having a significant positive or negative impact.

Seventh, the cultural context or environment might be the target. This category takes in a broad range of possible foci related to either the interviewer or interviewee that might be significant.

Intentional focusing implies that interviewers will deliberately select their targets for a reason and have a purpose in mind in the selection. A well-planned interview will move smoothly from one focus to another to establish a pattern of how these targets are related to one another in the client's life.

FOCUSING SKILLS: STAGES

Through selective focusing and directing you will bring out the complex issues being covered so that none of the important aspects will be ignored. You will increase the interviewee's awareness of the many factors involved, help to organize those factors appropriately, help to filter out confusion, and help to establish priorities. You will carefully observe the interviewee's needs to determine your focus and directives in the interview. It is important to make a deliberate and intentional choice in your focus, so that the interview does not wander at random. You will have a plan to follow, and you will have back-up plans in case the counseling does not proceed as anticipated. You will want to move from one focus to another in helping the interviewee organize the situation and find new behaviors to fulfill the original culturally learned and valued expectations.

Through selective focusing you are now at the stage of integrating the culture-centered counseling skills covered in this book. The next step is to practice so that you will become more comfortable and spontaneous in your ability to use them.

In focusing, interpreting, and directing counseling the first step is to structure skills to meet the client's needs. Remembering that the client's needs are defined by culturally learned expectations and values, that means coming to understand those expectations and values as the client understands them. The basic listening sequence of encouraging, paraphrasing, and summarizing will help the counselor. Questioning, reflecting feeling or meaning, and doing a positive asset search allow the counselor to build on what was learned through listening and to try different strategies with the client. Ivey suggests that a typical interview structure emphasizing attending skills will follow five stages, adapted to the four synthetic cultures.

Stage 1: Establishing Rapport and Relationship Building

Alpha agenda. To show respect for the hierarchy of power, to be polite and not rushed, to listen carefully until invited to give an opinion, to remain restrained and formal.

Beta agenda. To identify clear goals and realistic objectives, to work within the structure and rules of Beta culture, to provide a detailed plan with favorable outcomes.

Gamma agenda. To allow flexibility and open alternatives, to define shared self-interests of participants, to respect individual freedom and dignity needs, to be creative and innovative.

Delta agenda. To demonstrate a successful track record, to reward assertiveness and competition, to emphasize the profit motive, to reward merit and risk-taking by participants.

Stage 2: Gathering Data and Information

Alpha agenda. Listen and observe, rather than ask lots of questions, allow Alpha leaders to control information, be patient, even if getting required information takes time, don't be pushy in forcing your agenda on Alphas.

Beta agenda. Develop categories and a structure to organize each specific detail you collect, be accurate and careful in managing data, work within the rules, do not surprise a Beta with unexpected questions or actions.

Gamma agenda. Gather your information from individuals outside of groups, expect conflicting and contradictory perceptions, be careful not to take sides in controversy, try to demonstrate how cooperation is in the Gamma's best self-interest.

Delta agenda. Do not threaten Deltas, but be direct and pushy in pursuing your agenda, expect data and information that describes Deltas favorably, be careful gathering unfavorable data, demonstrate daring and risk-taking through clever strategies in getting insider information.

Stage 3: Developing a Plan for Determining Outcomes

Alpha agenda. Work within the socially defined roles appropriate to Alphas, protect and strengthen the hierarchy if possible, protect and strengthen harmony in Alpha society, follow protocol and guidelines established by Alpha leaders, be humble and allow Alpha leaders to take credit for good ideas.

Beta agenda. Present a careful and detailed plan with clearly defined methods and realistically favorable outcomes, project consequences of alternatives, anticipate contingencies, respect rules of truth and law, work within the constraints of socially defined duty.

Gamma agenda. Present a broad and loosely defined plan where individual objectives complement one another, identify win-win outcomes in everyone's best self-interest, respect individual freedom and dignity, work around rules and obligations creatively, emphasize short-term goals.

Delta agenda. Be success-oriented and assertive in arguing for your viewpoint, focus on bottom-line profits and materialistic advantages, build in rewards and incentives for deserving behavior, favor a flashy and exciting presentation of your plan, don't be afraid to take chances.

Stage 4: Generating Alternative Solutions

Alpha agenda. Focus on traditional and conservative solutions within the hierarchy, be respectful in favoring solutions suggested by Alpha leaders, accept smaller and more modest alternatives that favor adjustment to the system, depend on Alpha counterparts to help generate appropriate solutions.

Beta agenda. Do your homework to make sure your solution is appropriate before presenting it, attend to detailed information and supporting data in defending your suggested alternative, anticipate difficult and even critical questions without becoming defensive.

Gamma agenda. Make sure that everybody wins and nobody loses, respect turf issues of personal privilege and expertise, try not to make enemies who might sabotage your solution, expect to debate and argue aggressively for your viewpoint, keep your cool under pressure, maintain control.

Delta agenda. Demonstrate how your solution works better than any alternatives, assert your viewpoint, push for a positive decision, take on the opposition directly but with clever strategies to co-opt arguments, use sports metaphors in describing your solutions.

Stage 5: Generalizing and Transferring Learning

Alpha agenda. Work from a consensus, however long it takes, so that everyone supports your idea before your move, involve the Alpha leaders in essential aspects of implementing your plan, keep a low profile, give credit to others if your plan is successful.

Beta agenda. Try out your ideas in a smaller pilot project before you implement it in total, keep careful records to demonstrate the success or failure of your plan, develop back-up plans that anticipate any negative contingency, move slowly and carefully in transferring learning to the real world.

Gamma agenda. Promote individual change to achieve higher levels of excellence, highlight the new and innovative ideas in your plan and how it will improve society, follow up all levels of the plan as it is implemented from a great variety of viewpoints.

Delta agenda. Demonstrate how your plan guarantees success and winning outcomes, highlight and promote successful aspects of the plan, advertise the plan widely and with a high visibility, eliminate the opposition in any way necessary, use the "old boys" network, call in debts that others owe you to help you succeed.

FOCUSING SKILLS: SALIENCE

Focusing, interpreting, and directing go beyond basic attending skills to describe a more active counselor role in taking control or directing the interview in one direction or another, consciously and deliberately. As you have already experienced with the four synthetic cultures, each is complex in its perspective, requiring a unique focus. However, each culture is also dynamic, as the salient cultural perspective keeps changing from time to time and place to place.

Culture is defined as complex and dynamic (Pedersen, 1988). This means not only that each person belongs to many different cultures according to ethnographic, demographic, status, and affiliations, but also that not all those cultures are equally important all the time. The culture-centered counselor will need to track salience as it moves from one to another culture or social-system variable in the client's background. We have discussed focusing skills in terms of targets and in terms of stages. Now we turn to focusing as a process of directing and redirecting attention to the salient features of a client's multicultural background. The task of focusing on salience is a dynamic process that requires a profound awareness of the client's many cultures as well as those cues a client gives to suggest a shift in attention from one feature to another.

Focusing on salience is directly related to the allocation and use of power in the interview. To the extent that a counselor wishes to take more power and control, he or she will direct or redirect the focus of the interview. As the client develops more power and control, he or she may take full responsibility for identifying salience. The intentional use of focusing is intended to facilitate client growth and development in culturally appropriate ways to identify and explore salience with a minimum of intervention by the counselor or others. Focusing shifts attention from less relevant to more relevant topics in counseling which encourage the client to take more responsibility and risks within the safety of the interview. Focusing skills become the "steering wheel" of counseling, as the interview moves toward the destination of success.

Focusing becomes particularly difficult in culture-centered counseling. The counselor and client are typically bound by different rules of behavior and learned expectations in multicultural settings. Common ground becomes more difficult to identify in multicultural settings. Culture-centered counselors not only need to focus on the client's salient culture, but also dare not be distracted by their own contrasting salience. All of the microskills previously discussed in this book are required for the difficult task of focusing in a multicultural setting.

The role of culture-centered focusing is to keep track of the salient cultural perspective of values or expectations as they change from one moment or situation to the next. We have already discussed culture as complex, dynamic, but fundamental to understanding either the client or the counselor. If a client comes in a wheelchair to see me and I presume that the client's problems relate to disability, I may miss the changing perspective as salience moves to gender, ethnicity, life-style, or other affiliations. The obvious culture may not be salient, and the salient culture may not be obvious—as indicated in Exercise 10.1.

EXERCISE 10.1: FOCUSING ON SALIENCE

This exercise is designed to help you practice your skills in focusing on the complex and dynamic salient cultural features of a client's presenting problem.

1. Obtain a transcript of a counseling interview from a standard text or classroom activity. A videotaped counseling interview would be even better.
2. Study the transcript in detail to identify verbal and nonverbal behaviors that remind you of Alpha (high power distance), Beta (strong uncertainty avoidance), Gamma (individualistic), or Delta (strongly masculine).
3. Write down at least three or four examples of each synthetic culture in the behavior of the client and/or counselor in the interview.
4. Discuss your examples with those your partner located to see if you observed the same or different features.
5. Discuss how this information might be helpful as you track the changing salience of a client's complex culture in a counseling interview.

DIRECTING SKILLS

Directives are also important skills for influencing a client's behavior. Directives generally include suggestions, advice, or requests and may range from casual and indirect hints to an uncompromising order with consequences. The directive is usually given to help the client achieve preferred consequences, usually with some rationale or interpretation that helps the client understand why the counselor is directing a particular action or behavior.

Giving directives involves taking on responsibility. It puts the counselor in the role of a teacher imparting new information as a source of wisdom. In many cultures counseling is frequently done by persons in a teaching role, and the efficacy of a counselor is judged by the truth and wisdom of his or her teachings. In these cultures a counselor who relies exclusively on reflection with little or no influencing, directing, or focusing might well be judged as incompetent or unwise, with nothing new to teach the client.

In the same mode a counselor who self-discloses his or her ignorance about the client's culture in a culture that views counseling as a form of teaching might make the client wonder why he or she came to that counselor in the first place. Directives work best when there is a basic foundation of trust and respect so that the counselor already has credibility with the client.

Ivey (1988) suggests that a more directive interview might include the following three steps:

1. First, the counselor needs to listen, observe, and attend carefully to understand the client's situation and cultural context. This may require patience and a high level of pattern-recognition skill to see how each behavior is related to culturally learned expectations and values and ultimately to a network of social-system variables.

2. Second, the counselor needs to assess the client's needs and the opportunities available in that cultural context. Perhaps this will mean identifying different behaviors that can more appropriately and effectively fulfill positive cultural expectations and values. The counselor will teach the client something of value through influencing, directing, or focusing on salient features.

3. Third, the counselor will follow up the influencing intervention with the client to see if the new teachings worked or not. If the new teachings can be related to old positive values, then there is a greater possibility that the teachings will become a more permanent feature for the client.

Ivey (1988) also outlines fourteen directives frequently used that might be adapted for culture-centered counseling.

1. The counselor can advise or make specific suggestions for a particular action by the client at a particular time and place.

2. The counselor might use "paradoxical instructions" with clients that are resistant to other directions so they can experience the logical consequences of their behaviors.

3. Counselors might suggest using imagery to visualize a situation or to explore metaphors in counseling.

4. Counselors might use role-play to help clients see the situation as a participant, rather than as an objective and passive observer.

5. Counselors might use a "gestalt hot seat," getting clients to take on the role of significant others to understand better their viewpoints in the here and now.

6. Counselors might use "gestalt nonverbals" to help the client articulate the affective or less cognitive aspects of a problem.

7. Counselors might ask clients to free-associate in a psychodynamic mode to understand better the historical background of a problem.

8. Counselors might use positive reframing of a situation to help the client locate sources of support and resources for dealing with problems.

9. Counselors might use relaxation to help clients understand the physiological impact of their problems.

10. Counselors might use systematic desensitization to help the client move from higher to lower levels of anxiety.

11. The counselor might change the words or vocabulary a client uses as a means of changing a client's perception.

12. Counselors might advocate meditation to access internal self-righting resources of the mind and body to deal with problems.

13. Counselors might involve the family as a source of information and support to a more collectivist client.

14. Counselors might advocate some sort of homework that involves the client as a participant in the counseling process.

There are, of course, many additional directives that might be used in a variety of different ways at different times and places. There is a danger that these directives might result in what Wrenn (1962, 1985) described as "cultural encapsulation." The culturally encapsulated counselor substitutes stereotypes for the real world, disregards cultural variations among clients, and dogmatizes technique-oriented definitions of counseling. There is always the danger that a counselor might use directives to impose her or his own self-reference cultural perspective.

Most counselors or therapists around the world use similar directives or patterns of help-giving. Torrey (1986) went so far as to draw direct parallels between the techniques of witch doctors and psychiatrists in: naming their treatment, identifying a cause, establishing rapport, developing client expectation for improvement, and demonstrating legitimacy. There is a disarming degree of similarity in presenting problems across cultures.

The same problems of depression, loneliness, anger, difficulty in relationships, low self-image, and distracted thinking, for example, can be found in most, if not all, cultures. However, the appropriate response to these similar problems is almost certainly going to be different from one cultural setting to another. It is dangerous to assume that the same problem will require the same solution across cultures. Thus, while the act of directing/teaching/focusing might be a universal in counseling, and the kind of problem may also be a universal, the appropriate response to that problem is almost certainly unique to a particular time, place, and person.

EXERCISE 10.2: USING DIRECTIVE SKILLS WITH SYNTHETIC CULTURES

The objective of this exercise is to practice a variety of different directives or advice giving to clients from different cultural backgrounds who seem to be encountering the same problem.

1. Select a particular presenting problem such as loneliness, divorce, failure in school, drug usage, or pregnancy. Write that universal presenting problem here:

2. Identify directives or words of advice that you believe might be appropriate for clients from the four synthetic cultures, each of whom is experiencing the same problem.

   Alpha directive:

   Beta directive:

   Gamma directive:

   Delta directive:

3. Compare your directives with those of others in your group.

4. Discuss the strengths and weakness of each directive for each synthetic culture.

INTERPRETING SKILLS

There are three questions the culture-centered counselor needs to ask in order to interpret the client accurately (Cormier and Cormier, 1991).

First, how deep do you want to go in your interpretation? Think of depth as the degree of difference between what the client believes to be true and what the counselor believes to be true. If you present a client with a viewpoint that is a little different from the client's own, the client might accept it and make the necessary change. However, if the difference is too great, the client is almost certain to reject the contrasting viewpoint completely. The counselor needs to decide just how much change can be made at one time. If the necessary change is made too quickly, counseling will fail. If the necessary change is made too slowly, counseling will also fail. When the counselor and client are from different cultures, the discrepancy is likely to be considerable, and there is the greater risk that the counselor as well as the client will need to make changes.

Second, what direction or focus do you want to take in your interpretation? If you focus on factors within the client's control, you are likely to be more successful. Focusing on factors outside the client's control is not likely to be successful. Clients with a more internal locus of control will present a larger target for focusing, while clients with a more external locus will require a more sharply defined focus to detect salient social-system variables.

Third, what is the positive or negative connotation of your interpretation? Interpretations imply value judgments, either explicitly or implicitly, of the client by the counselor. For that reason interpretations require a high level of skill to be done accurately and appropriately. Culturally different clients are especially likely to be judged and to make judgements in culture-centered counseling. Positive interpretations are more likely to bring about change than negative interpretations, even though negative interpretations that a culturally different client forms may sometimes be necessary.

Focusing and directing combine and build on all the previous culture-centered counseling skills. By now you should have developed some insight into your own preferred style of counseling in terms of the culturally learned values and expectations behind your behaviors. You should also have identified at least four contrasting cultural groups—through the synthetic cultures—where those same or similar expectations and values might be expressed by different preferred counseling behaviors. This is the beginning of a framework for counseling in a multicultural setting.

The function of interpretation is to provide a new perspective to the client. Accurate and appropriate interpretation serves to clarify problem(s) and to identify new choices or alternatives for the client. In culture-centered counseling interpretation requires the counselor to be aware of her or his own cultural assumptions as well as the contrasting assumptions of a culturally different client. The counselor might reframe the interpretation in terms that are appropriate to the client's culture so that it will be heard and might lead to constructive change. Reframing might involve changing the words used to make the interpretation, modifying the process of interpretation according to the client's communication style, and linking the interpretation to the client's salient cultures. The interpretation might require translation to the client's culture much in the same way that language might require translation—so that it will be accurately understood and have an appropriate effect.

If you are working with a lonely client, for example, how would you interpret that loneliness differently according to whether the client was an Alpha, Beta, Gamma, or Delta? How would you reframe the same interpretation in ways that might be sensitive but still effective? For an Alpha client you might, for example, emphasize the client's sure and certain role in the Alpha hierarchy and a sense of belonging. For a Beta client you might emphasize the specific situations that result in loneliness and specific actions that have been proven effective to reduce loneliness in others. For a Gamma client you might emphasize the positive features of loneliness, such as freedom, independence, and a frontier spirit of individuality. For a Delta client you might emphasize loneliness as the price of success or that it is "lonely at the top." In each case loneliness would be interpreted differently in order to interpret accurately. Culture-centered counseling skills provide guidelines for interpreting culturally different clients' behaviors in accurate and appropriate ways.

SUMMARY

In order to summarize focusing, directing, and interpreting skills it is important to review the five stages of counseling mentioned earlier, which provide the structure to apply what we have learned.

With regard to developing rapport you should be able to listen and observe carefully enough to identify the communication patterns of preference for the client's culture. Imagine that the client is defining a pool of words, behaviors, and concepts for you as you listen. You are now free to draw from those words, behaviors, and concepts as you interact, but you are not free to introduce new words, behaviors, and concepts.

By working within the client's words, behaviors, and concepts you will begin working from within the client's culturally learned perspective. Restricting yourself in this way will be awkward at first but can become easier with practice. The goal and objective is to earn the culturally different client's trust and respect by demonstrating a willingness to work within a conceptual perspective.

It may take longer to establish rapport than you are accustomed to in your own culture, especially if you are working with clients who have had a bad experience with other counselors from your culture. Learning patience can be important. What you do not do will be interpreted as well as what you do in many cultures where nothing happens by accident. Everything you do and everything that you do not do will be considered in the client's decision to accept or reject you. Foreign students frequently describe Americans as "friendly . . . but I have no friends!"

With regard to defining the problem and summarizing the assets available to the client, it is important to escape from the self-reference criterion. Do not do onto others as you would have them do onto you, because they might want something different. It is very easy and automatic to use one's self as the measure of what others want and why they do what they do, but this will almost always be misleading. You can overcome the temptation of the self-reference criterion only with considerable and persistent effort.

If you have gained entrance into the client's cultural perspective in the process of establishing rapport, you will discover aspects of the problem that you may not have thought about previously. In many cultures problems are externalized almost like demonic possession so that they are both good and bad, not just bad; active and always changing, not passive; complex—like a personality—and not simple. In other cultures the whole notion of "problem" implying a weakness is unacceptable, so a foreign student might admit to all sorts of difficulties but deny having any "problems."

From within the client's viewpoint you will also identify assets and resources upon which a culturally different client might draw. In many cultures a troubled person might first go inside him- or herself to the teachings or proverbs learned as a child to access an internalized counselor. Only when that internalized resource has failed might the client approach outsiders.

Clients in many cultures are surrounded by support systems of persons living and dead who might be called on to help and whom the counselor should never ignore. These support systems are a potentially valuable ally or a formidable enemy of the counselor, depending on how the counselor relates to them. Within the rules of each culture there will be special opportunities and restrictions that will dramatically shape available resources and assets for counseling.

In defining outcomes of counseling it is especially important to understand the client's cultural context. Some counselors can be accused of "scratching where it doesn't itch" when they offer inappropriate solutions. A counselor who is aware first of his or her own cultural values, second of the client's cultural values, and third of the similarities or differences between the counselor and the client is well prepared to define appropriate outcomes.

Appropriate outcomes define the goals of good counseling and will describe a plan for the counseling process. Pedersen (1988) describes culturally biased assumptions frequently found in counseling that are inappropriate across all cultures. Typically biased assumptions include the following imposed perspectives:

1. The notion that there is one universally accepted form of normality suggests that less powerful cultures conform to the ways of more powerful cultures, who define social norms.

2. The notion that individualism is healthier than collectivism is not valid in most of the world's populations.

3. Establishing artificial boundaries of discipline, expertise, and attention will prevent counselors from understanding complex and dynamic cultural problems.

4. Dependence on abstract jargon by low-context cultures puts counselors at a disadvantage when working with high-context clients.

5. The psychological stigma attached to dependent behavior is not accepted in many more collectivist cultures.

6. The tendency to ignore a person's natural support systems and deal with a client in isolation gives only a partial view of that culturally grounded client.

7. In attending to the culturally biased content of thinking it is also necessary to consider the cultural biased process of cause-effect, linear thinking when applied to nonlinear thinkers.

8. The emphasis on adjusting individuals to fit the system tends to protect the status quo against individuals, even when the individual is right and the system is wrong.

9. The disregard for history of individuals and cultures does a disservice to cultures in which history is important.

10. The presumption that one is free of cultural bias is the most dangerous assumption of all.

These widely accepted but culturally biased assumptions are likely to influence outcomes of multicultural counseling in the wrong direction.

The next stage in a counseling plan involves exploring alternatives and confronting incongruity. Here, again, culturally biased assumptions are likely to shape the perspectives and perceptions that define alternatives and indicate incongruity. Frequently the client will have some ideas of alternatives that they either have tried or thought about. The client may be brought into counseling as a "consultant" and participate in defining viable alternatives. In any case, there will be constraints and opportunities for each different cultural setting that will require attention.

It is important to define and identify common-ground values and expectations that bring together different persons in each situation, including the counselor and client themselves. Different behaviors can become acceptable as long as the deeper values and expectations are preserved. As the counselor identifies incongruity it might be more important to focus on expectations than on behaviors. Apparent incongruities might in actuality disguise shared expectations in spite of different behaviors. It is important not to be distracted by behaviors—no matter how discrepant they might seem—until they are understood from the viewpoint of the client's values and expectations.

The fifth stage of generalizing from the counseling setting to the real world is the most difficult of all. When the client leaves the artificiality of a counseling setting and returns to the real-life pressures of situations that originally gave rise to the problems, the rules change. Rules that work in the counseling interview might not work in the real world, just as rules from the real world might not work in counseling.

The counselor has taught the client a new role in a new context. Steenbarger (1991) describes the importance of social role theory in a developmental context, showing how we construct our own realities. We are created out of our social interactions, and we ourselves participate in that creation. The counseling context simply becomes one more role the client has learned as appropriate for a particular context. To assume that every client will become a missionary for this newly learned role in other contexts would be naive and dangerous.

It is useful for counselors working with other cultures to explore informal counseling methods and contexts that are less tied to an office or a schedule and are more spontaneous to the formal/informal, structured/unstructured perspectives of our clients.

Culture-centered counseling is an attempt to focus on the culturally learned rules by which we have each constructed our own reality. From the perspective of these complex and dynamic culturally learned rules it becomes possible to track the changing salience of problems, persons, and situations across cultures. This book has attempted to identify a series of skills that have also been identified by other skill-based books on counseling. Those skills have been modified to fit the contrasting requirements of four synthetic cultures to help readers increase their repertoire of how each might be appropriately used in multicultural settings. As all counselors become more culture-centered it will be possible to incorporate a multicultural perspective into counseling as a discipline.

The basic underlying message of this book is that culture is important because that's where the power is. Counseling that disregards cultural similarities and differences is unlikely to be accurate and effective except to impose the will and rules of a more powerful group on less powerful groups. Culture-centered counseling is presented as an obvious and practical approach for translating the growth opportunities of counseling to the whole world of culturally different peoples.

KEY IDEAS

1. The purpose of focusing skills.
   Helps identify different viewpoints on the same topic.
   Guides the interview toward specific goals.
   Regulates or changes emphasis in the interview.
   Increases the interviewee's ability to focus on the problem appropriately.

2. Focusing skills: targets.
   The interviewee.
   The main topic/theme/problem.
   The interviewer.
   Other persons.
   The family.
   The relationship between interviewer and interviewee.
   The culture/environment/context.

3. Focusing skills: stages.
   Establishing rapport and relationship building.
   Gathering data and information.
   Developing a plan for determining outcomes.
   Generating alternative solutions.
   Generalizing and transferring learning.

4. Focusing skills: salience.
   Focusing is a dynamic and active process.
   Salience changes from one focus to another in the interview.
   Focusing is difficult in multicultural interviews.
   Tracking salience is an important focusing skill.

5. Directing skills.
   Directives include suggestions, advice, and requests.
   Giving directives means accepting responsibility.
   Directives work best when there is trust.
   Directives involve listening, assessing, and intervention.

Ivey's list of fourteen different directives.
Wrong directives may be culturally encapsulated.
The problems are similar but solutions are different.

6. Interpreting skills.
   How deep do you want to go in your interpretation?
   What direction do you want to take?
   What is the positive or negative connotation?
   Interpretation provides a new perspective.
   Interpretation must be reframed for each cultural setting.

7. Summary.
   How do you develop rapport with a different culture?
   How do you define a culturally different problem?
   How do you know what outcome is culturally appropriate?
   How do you identify culturally appropriate alternatives?
   How do you transfer insight in culturally appropriate ways?
   Culture-centered counseling means learning different rules.
   Culture-centered counseling means adapting skills.
   Culture-centered counseling means going with the power.

10.3: EXERCISE IN FOCUSING, DIRECTING, AND INTERPRETING

Select two partners to form a three-person group including an interviewer, an interviewee from one of the four synthetic cultures, and an observer for a ten-minute role-played interview.

Before the interview ask the client to identify at least three of the following targets for the counselor to focus on: the interviewee, the topic/theme/problem, the interviewer, others, the counseling relationship, the family, the culture/environment/context. The counselor will seek to identify each of these selected targets as it becomes salient in the interview.

During the interview the interviewer will attempt to move from stage one (establishing rapport) to stage two (gathering data and information) up to stage three (identifying goals and outcomes). Explain and identify each shift from one stage to another to your client.

At the end of the interview the observer will provide directions in terms of suggestions, advice, or requests based on material that came up during the interview.

After the interview the counselor and the client will, in five minutes, independently write down their interpretation of the interview in terms of the differences between the interviewer and interviewee, the most important factors on which the interview should have focused, and their evaluation of the strengths and weaknesses of the other.

Discuss the interview and share the written interpretation.

Instructions to the observer: Listen and watch for specific examples of focusing skills as they are used in the interview.

1. Identified complex issues.
   Example:

2. Increased the interviewee's awareness of many factors.
   Example:

3. Organized factors appropriately.
   Example:

4. Reduced confusion in the interview.
   Example:

5. Established priorities in the interview.
   Example:

6. Made transitions smoothly from one focus to another.
   Example:

References

Amir, Y. 1969. Contact hypothesis in ethnic relations. *Psychological Bulletin* 71:319–42.

Astin, M. I. 1978. *Management simulations for mental health and human service administration.* New York: Haworth Press.

Baker, S., and Daniels, T. 1989. Integrating research on the microcounseling program: A meta-analysis. *Journal of Counseling Psychology* 35:213–22.

Baker, S., Daniels, T., and Greeley, A. 1990. Systematic training of graduate-level counselors: Narrative and meta-analytic reviews of three major programs. *Counseling Psychologist* 18:355–421.

Barna, L. M. 1982. Stumbling blocks in intercultural communication. In *Intercultural communication: A reader*, ed. L. Samovar and R. Porter, 330–38. Belmont, CA: Wadsworth.

Berry, J. W. 1969. On cross cultural comparability. *International Journal of Psychology* 4:119–28.

Bieri, J. 1955. Cognitive complexity, simplicity, and predictive behavior. *Journal of Abnormal and Social Psychology* 51:263–68.

Blanchard, F. 1991. Experiment in psychology at Smith College, Northampton MA. Unpublished document.

Brammer, L. M. 1988. *The helping relationship: Process and skills.* Englewood Cliffs, NJ: Prentice-Hall.

Brislin, R. S., et al. 1986. *Intercultural interactions: A practical guide.* Beverly Hills, CA: Sage.

Brislin, R.; Landis, D.; and Brandt, M. 1983. Conceptualizations of intercultural behavior and training. In *Handbook of intercultural training*, ed. D. Landis and R. Brislin. Vol. 1, *Issues in theory and design*, 1–36. New York: Pergamon.

Brunner, J. S. 1990. *Acts of meaning.* Cambridge, MA: Harvard University Press.

Burger, J. M. 1990. *Personality.* Belmont, CA: Wadsworth.

Corey, G. 1991. *Theory and practice of counseling and psychotherapy.* Pacific Grove, CA: Brooks Cole.

Cormier, W. H., and Cormier L. S. 1991. *Interviewing strategies for helpers.* Pacific Grove, CA: Brooks Cole.

Crockett, W. H. 1965. Cognitive complexity and impression formation. In *Progress in experimental personality research*, ed. B. A. Maher. Vol. 2. New York: Academic Press.

Daniels, T. 1985. *Microcounseling: Training in skills of therapeutic communication with R.N. department program nursing students.* Unpublished doctoral dissertation, Dalhousie University, Halifax, Nova Scotia.

Dillon, J. T. 1990. *The practice of questioning.* New York: Routledge.

Duryea, M. L. 1992. *Conflict and culture: A literature review and bibliography.* Victoria, Can.: UVic Institute for Dispute Resolution.

Egan, G. 1985. *Change agent skills in helping and human service settings.* Monterey, CA: Brooks Cole.

———. 1986. *The skilled helper.* Monterey, CA: Brooks Cole.

———. 1990. *The skilled helper: Model, skills and methods for effective helping.* 4th ed. Pacific Grove, CA: Brooks Cole.

Ellis, A. 1977. The basic clinical theory of rational-emotive therapy. In *Handbook of rational-emotive therapy,* ed. A. Ellis and R. Greiger. Vol. 1, 3–34. New York: Springer.

Erickson, F., and Schultz, J. 1982. *The counselor as gatekeeper: Social interaction in interviews.* New York: Academic Press.

Fohs, M. 1982. Tape transcript submitted for credit. Syracuse University. Unpublished manuscript.

Frankl, V. 1963. *Man's search for meaning.* Boston: Beacon Press.

Goldstein, A. 1981. *Psychological skill training: The structural learning technique.* New York: Pergamon.

Goldstein, A., and Rosenbaum, A. 1982. *Aggress-Less: How to turn anger and aggression into positive action.* Englewood Cliffs, NJ: Prentice-Hall.

Goldstein, A., and Segall, M., eds. 1983. *Aggression in global perspective.* Elmsford, NY: Pergamon.

Goldstein, A. P., and Michaels, G. Y. 1985. *Empathy: Development training and consequences.* Hillside, NJ: Lawrence Earlbaum.

Goldstein, S. 1986. *Cultural issues in mediation: A literature review.* P.C.R. Working Paper, University of Hawaii, Honolulu.

Hermans, H. J. M.; Kempen, H. J. G.; and Van Loon, R. J. P. 1992. The dialogical self: Beyond individualism and rationalism. *American Psychologist* 47(1):23–33.

Hines, A., and Pedersen, P. 1982. The cultural grid: Management guidelines for a personal cultural orientation. *The Cultural Learning Institute Report.* March. Honolulu: East-West Center.

Hofstede, G. 1980. *Cultures consequences: International differences in work related values.* Beverly Hills, CA: Sage Publications.

———. 1986. Cultural differences in teaching and learning. *International Journal of Intercultural Relations* 10(3):301–20.

———. 1991. *Cultures and organizations: Software of the mind.* London: McGraw Hill.

Inkeles, A., and Levinson, D. J. 1969. National character: The study of modal personality and sociocultural systems. In *The handbook of social psychology,* ed. G. Lindsey and E. Aronson. 2d ed. Vol. 4, Reading, MA: Addison Wesley.

Ivey, A. 1971. *Microcounseling: Innovations in interviewing training.* Springfield, IL: Charles C Thomas.

Ivey, A., and Authier, J. 1978. *Microcounseling: Innovations in interviewing, counseling, psychotherapy, and psychoeducation.* 2d ed. Springfield, IL: Charles C Thomas.

Ivey, A. E. 1988. *Intentional interviewing and counseling: Facilitating client development.* Pacific Grove, CA: Brooks Cole.

———. 1991. *Developmental strategies for helpers of individual, family, and network interventions.* Pacific Grove, CA: Brooks Cole.

Ivey, A. E., and Galvin, M. 1982. Skills training: A model for treatment. In *Interpersonal helping skills,* ed. E. K. Marshall and P. D. Kurtz, 471–81. San Francisco: Jossey-Bass.

Ivey, A. E., Ivey, M. B., and Simek-Morgan, L. 1993. *Counseling and psychotherapy: A multicultural perspective.* Boston: Allyn and Bacon.

Janosik, R. J. 1987. Rethinking the culture-negotiation link. *Negotiation Journal* October:385–94.

Kagan, N., and McQuellon, R. 1981. Interpersonal process recall. In *Handbook of innovative psychotherapies*, ed. R. Corsini. New York: Wiley.

Kanfer, F. H., and Goldstein, A. P. 1986. *Helping people change: A textbook of methods, third edition.* New York: Pergamon.

Keefe, T. 1976. Empathy: The critical skill. *Social Work 21*:10–14.

Kelly, G. 1955. *The psychology of personal constructs.* New York: Norton.

Kurtz, P. D., and Marshall, E. K. 1982. *Interpersonal helping skills.* San Francisco: Jossey-Bass.

LeVine, R., and Campbell, D. C. 1972. *Ethnocentrism: Theories of conflict, ethnic attitudes and group behavior.* New York: Wiley.

Miller, N., and Brewer, M. B. 1984. *Groups in contact: The psychology of desegregation.* New York: Academic Press.

Nwachuku, U., and Ivey, A. 1991. Culture specific counseling: An alternative approach. *Journal of Counseling and Development 70*:106–11.

Pande, S. K. 1968. The mystique of Western psychotherapy: An Eastern interpretation. *Journal of Nervous and Mental Disease 146*:425–32.

Pedersen, A. 1985. Personal communication.

———. 1985. Unpublished exercise developed for a training workshop in Australia for the ADAB International.

Pedersen, A., and Pedersen, P. 1985. The cultural grid: A personal cultural orientation. In *Intercultural communication: A reader*, ed. L. Samovar and R. Porter, 50–62. Belmont CA: Wadsworth.

Pedersen, P. 1981. *Developing interculturally skilled counselors (DISC).* Final report to N.I.M.H. Honolulu: University of Hawaii.

———. 1982. The intercultural context of counseling and therapy. In *Cultural conceptions of mental health and therapy*, ed. A. Marsella and G. White, 333–58. Dordrecht, Holland: D. Reidel.

———. 1986. Developing interculturally skilled counselors: A training program. In *Cross-cultural training of mental health professionals*, ed. H. Lefley and P. Pedersen. Springfield, IL: Charles C Thomas.

———. 1988. *A handbook for developing multicultural awareness.* Alexandria, VA: American Association for Counseling and Development.

———. 1990. The constructs of complexity and balance in multicultural counseling theory and practice. *Journal of Counseling and Development 68*:550–54.

Pedersen, P., Draguns, J. G., Lonner, W. J., and Trimble, J. E. 1989. *Counseling across cultures.* 3d ed. Honolulu: University of Hawaii Press.

Pedersen, P., and Pedersen A. 1989. The cultural grid: A complicated and dynamic approach to multicultural counseling. *Counseling Psychology Quarterly 2*:133–41.

Pedersen, P., and Sprafkin R. 1986. *Basic multicultural skills: A synthetic culture training approach.* Syracuse, NY: Center for Instructional Development.

Pike, K. L. 1967. *Language in relation to a unified theory of the structure of human behavior.* The Hague: Mouton.

Rogers, C. 1951. *Client centered therapy.* Boston: Houghton Mifflin.

Rubin, J. Z.; Kim, S. H.; and Peretz, N. M. 1990. Expectancy effects and negotiation. *Journal of Social Issues 46*(2):125–39.

Sampson, E. E. 1989. The challenge of social change for psychology: Globalization and psychology's theory of the person. *American Psychologist 44*:914–21.

Sanders, N. M. 1966. *Classroom questions: What kinds?* New York: Harper and Row.

Segall, M. H. 1986. Culture and behavior: Psychology in global perspective. *Annual Review of Psychology* 37:523–64.

Segall, M. H., Dasen, P. R., Berry, J. W., and Poortinga, Y. H. 1990. *Human behavior in global perspective.* New York: Pergamon.

Spradley, J. P. 1976. *Cross cultural research: The ethnographic interview.* Prepared for a National Science Foundation project, Macalester College, St. Paul.

Steenbarger, B. N. 1991. All the world is not a stage: Emerging contextualist themes in counseling and development. *Journal of Counseling and Development* 70(2):288–96.

Stewart, E. 1971. *American cultural patterns: A cross cultural perspective.* Pittsburgh: Regional Council for International Understanding.

Sue, D. W., Bernier, J. E., Durran, A., Feinberg, L., Pedersen, P., Smith, C. J., and Vasquez-Nuttall, G. 1982. Cross cultural counseling competencies. *The Counseling Psychologist* 19(2):45–54.

Sue, D. W., and Sue, D. 1990. *Counseling the culturally different: Theory and practice.* New York: Wiley.

Sunoo, J. J. M. 1990. Some guidelines for mediators of intercultural disputes. *Negotiation Journal* October:383–89.

Tetlock, P. E. 1985. Integrative complexity of American and Soviet foreign policy rhetoric: A time series analysis. *Journal of Personality and Social Psychology* 49:1565–85.

Thelen, H. A. 1956. *Dynamics of groups at work.* Chicago: University of Chicago Press.

Torrey, E. F. 1986. *Witchdoctors and psychiatrists: The common roots of psychotherapy and its future.* New York: Harper and Row.

Triandis, H. 1972. *The analysis of subjective culture.* New York: Wiley.

———. 1975. Social psychology and cultural analysis. *Journal for the Theory of Social Behavior* 5:81–106.

———. 1983. *Allocentric vs. idiocentric social behavior: A major cultural difference between Hispanics and the Mainstream.* ONR Technical Report 16. Champaign: University of Illinois, Department of Psychology.

Truax, C. B., and Carkhuff, R. R. 1967. *Toward effective counseling and psychotherapy.* Hawthorne, NY: Aldine.

Wehrly, B., and Watson-Gegeo, K. 1985. Ethnographic methodologies as applied to the study of cross cultural counseling. In *Handbook of cross-cultural counseling and therapy,* ed. P. Pedersen, 65–73. Westport, CT: Greenwood Press.

Wrenn, C. G. 1962. The culturally encapsulated counselor. *Harvard Educational Review* 32:444–49.

———. 1985. Afterword: The culturally encapsulated counselor revisited. In *Handbook of cross-cultural counseling and therapy,* ed. P. Pedersen, 323–31. Westport, CT: Greenwood Press.

Index

About the Authors

PAUL B. PEDERSEN is Professor of Education and Counseling Educator at Syracuse University. He is well known for his expertise in multicultural counseling. His previous books include *Handbook of Cross-Cultural Counseling and Therapy* (Greenwood Press, 1985).

ALLEN IVEY is Distinguished University Professor at the University of Masssachusetts at Amherst. An ABPP Diplomate and past President of the Division of Counseling Psychology of APA, he is the author of 20 books translated into 14 languages. His most recent work is *Counseling and Psychotherapy: A Multicultural Perspective* (1992).